THE GHOST DANCE

To Maité,
what a wonderful surprise
to meet like this.

Love

Michael Stuart

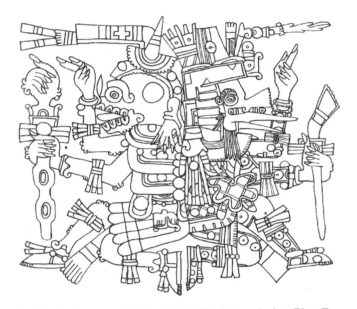

The Plumed Serpent and the Lord of the Dead dance the first Ghost Dance
-Codex Borgia

THE GHOST DANCE
An Untold History of the Americas

MICHAEL STUART ANI

I dedicate this book, The Ghost Dance, to the spirits of the wild and free in the hope that their wisdom can help us to maintain our place in the weave of nature.

TABLE OF CONTENTS

SECTION 3: THE PRESENT

CHAPTER 1
THE VELADA CEREMONY

The Mushroom Initiate

In that moment of silence between twilight and darkness, when the cloud forest's creatures of night awakened, I bolted shut the cedar door of the hacienda at Rancho Catalunya. The crumbling adobe walls stood alone, the ruins of a fortress in the peaks of the Sierra Mazateca of Oaxaca, Mexico. Long before the time of the Aztec, the Toltec sages came to these Mountains of the Clouds to worship the gods of their ancient ancestors. This was the place where the earth met the sky and the Ghost Dance began.

As darkness fell, I struck a match and lit a beeswax candle on a wooden altar covered with tropical wild flowers. I watched as copal smoke rose up from a clay incense burner in front of the flickering flame. Candlelight animated the bearded, bronze mask of the ancient god of fire, *Huehueteotl*, and his closed eyes opened with a quiver. In that sacred moment the usually noisy cloud forest went completely silent. Gazing into the crest of the flame, I humbly asked Grandfather Fire to call upon *Desheto*, the Prince of Plants, whose name was always whispered with the most profound reverence. When the frogs began to sing, I knew the old god had heard me and I continued the ghost ritual as I had learned it from *Desheto* himself.

I unwrapped a large banana leaf, the pungent fragrance of thirteen pairs of twisted fungi rose up. *Desheto* had told me that these sacred mushrooms were spawned from the seed of the Plumed Serpent at the first Ghost Dance and were called the Little Ones.

I asked the Little Ones' forgiveness for cutting their lives short while purifying them in the smoke of copal incense for their journey to the land of the dead. Then I ate them in pairs so their journey would not be lonely. Not a moment after I finished, I could hear a distant wind gently rustling the leaves of faraway trees and I whispered, *"Nina ski-tah chili."*

"The gods give to those who give to the gods."

After I extinguished the candle with the belled top of a flower, I sat in the darkness and listened as a far-off wind blew with a chilling howl. Wrapping myself in a *serape*, I curled up on a straw mat to warm my rattling bones. As my shivering subsided, my mind drifted back to the events that had brought me here. I had returned from the Great Jungle of the South where *Desheto* had sent me to shed my boyhood skin. Barely surviving the ordeal, I had returned to finish the Ghost Dance ritual that had begun in one of Mexico's most dangerous and remote regions. But I was not defenseless and alone this night, as the Clean Sisters kept a vigil on the other side of the crumbling patio.

The *Comadres Limpiadas* was a sisterhood based on cleanliness that had watched over the ghost ceremony since before the time of the Toltec. I could hear the Clean Sisters softly praying.

"Grandfather, I sit before you, a Daughter of the Moon, and a Clean Sister. Hummingbirds of Dreams, lead this dancer across the Milky Way."

The harmony between the Little Ones' singing inside me and the sisterhood's prayer was soothing, but my calm was disturbed when the bubbling notes of the Little Ones' song began to morph into chatter. It was as if the Little Ones were rushing to tell their life story before they died. But with so many voices chattering away at the same time, it was hard to grasp the urgency that grew with the beating pulse of a distant wind.

Beckoned by the untamed fury of this living wind, I stood up and opened the slatted shutters of the hacienda to a sky of churning clouds illuminated from behind by a blood moon. As a bolt of lightning cracked like a flashing serpent's tongue, it licked the dank underbellies of the clouds and ignited the Crucible of the Summer Storm.

A clap of thunder sent the whirling wind racing up the stone path towards Catalunya, gaining momentum until it reached the porch. Startled by the force of the wind, I quickly closed the shutters just before the wind slammed into the weathered wood with a mighty burst. The gust exploded into a flurry of iridescent Wind Serpents that slithered into the room through every available crack. As the Wind Serpents filled the darkness, they wove in and out of each other, forming a brilliant mosaic. From the center of this tapestry, a single Wind Serpent opened its mouth and lunged forward, baring its fangs and striking me unconscious.

When I awoke, the Wind Serpents were gone, but I could sense *Desheto* hiding in the shadows. He was so skittish I worried that one wrong move could scare him away, or worse, provoke a fierce attack. As I approached cautiously, we began a dance, moving back and forth like wild animals, a dance in which we both gained trust in the other but still kept up our guard.

For what seemed an eternity, my guest remained silent, but then he finally began to speak. At first, he whispered in an archaic tongue that I didn't comprehend, but as he continued, the Little Ones dying inside me began to act as translators.

"It is I, *Desheto*. It brings me great joy to see you, *Maguey*. I knew you'd come back."

"The task you gave me was not easy," I replied. "The jungle almost ate me alive, but the memory of your voice kept me going when I needed it most, even though I am still not sure who you really are."

Desheto spoke again. "I was a speck of dust blown across the universe like a vagabond upon the winds of time, and came to rest here in the clouds where the Ghost Dance began. I sent you out to become a man, *Maguey*. What did you learn from the Great Jungle of the South?"

I took a moment to compose my thoughts and speak the words I'd gone over in my head many times before while I lay awake at night in the jungle, listening to the roar of howler monkeys.

"When I first arrived at the edge of the jungle, I only dressed the part. I had few skills, but I did have the courage to continue on," I answered. "That courage, or false pride, whichever it was, led me through her gauntlet, broke me down to nothing, and shredded my jungle costume in the mud. Only when there was almost nothing left of the boy, did the jungle begin to heal me and change me into a creature who could survive under her canopy. The jungle breaks down your defenses and takes you on her terms, not yours. You have to change to survive; only then will she show you her secrets and make you strong."

I was very pleased with my explanation, but *Desheto* stirred in the darkness, unfulfilled, pushing me towards some deeper understanding.

"What else did you see, beyond your own self-importance?" *Desheto* pressed.

"What else did I see? The jungle and her creatures are endless like the oceans; Indians still hide behind every tree. The ancient way is very much alive. There are still spirits in the shadows who whisper your name, *Desheto*."

Exasperated by my self-indulgence, *Desheto* barked back, "Did you only see what you wanted to see while casting a blind eye to the fray at the edge of the world?"

Feeling the sharpness of his dismissal, I lashed back, "I'm not blind. I saw the disease, destruction and hunger in the jungle, but I chose to see life, not death! The jungle just seems to feed on everything, good and bad. That's her nature. Nothing can stop her."

Desheto paused for a long time before he spoke again, "Remember these words I speak to you now."

I felt a chill as the Prince of Plants began to speak, "Before you are an old man, the birds of the jungle will no longer blaze like fire across the sky. Mountains of ice at the top of the world will melt and the sea will rise and fall, poisoning its waters and claiming its shores. You did not see because you have not yet learned to see. Your kind, the Two-Legged Ones, have been tricked into destroying your strand in the weave of nature, but I have come to help you."

Even though *Desheto* had constantly reinforced my belief in him, doubt raised its ugly head and I began to question his wisdom. In 1972, the Great Jungle had appeared indestructible. At my tender age it was impossible for me to see an end; I was only aware of the beginning. Before I could stop him, *Desheto* continued his doomsday oration:

"Soon, no hollow, two-legged words of false leaders or experts to whom they pay trade shells to make their lies seem true will help the people, rich or poor. Only the Ghost Dance can save the Two-Legged Ones, but the steps to the dance have been lost."

In the past, *Desheto* had been a host of great joy and profound knowledge, but all this hopelessness pushed me over the edge. I decided to move past my fears, light the candle and finally, after all this time, see who spoke such strong words.

Covered by darkness, my hand gently moved across the altar until I felt the little box of matches. Removing a match, I went to strike it, but before I could, *Desheto* hissed, lightning crackled and thunder rumbled. Like wild beasts, the gods of the elements escalated their reaction to such a rage that I was certain the sky would fall at any moment and I would be just another ant crushed under its weight. I dropped the match and trembled, with my head turned down in submission, cursing my boyish foolery and begging for forgiveness.

Desheto appeared to be calmed by my sincere apology, and the elements subsided as quickly as they came. There was even a touch of remorse in his voice as *Desheto* explained his agenda.

"I have remained hidden for a very long time and it is true that hidden knowledge has a power of its own. It is also true that hidden knowledge meant to be used at a later date loses all its power unless it is brought out of hiding and used at precisely the right time. The completion of this cycle of the Ghost Dance is almost here and so it is time to tell the story that I have been petitioned by the Plumed Serpent to tell to the Two-Legged Ones, so they may never say that they did not know the steps needed to save their strand in the weave of nature."

With great humility, he continued, whispering softly, "I do not have hands that know how to write or a voice that can be spoken into a machine. You, *Maguey*, are *Ani*, Scribe to the Dead, and so you will be my hands and my voice. You will be my scribe, *Ani*. You will inscribe my story of the Ghost Dance."

Sheepishly, I replied, "Oh great Lord, forgive me but there really must be a mistake. I am barely literate, never mind a Scribe to the Dead."

Desheto rose up now, with joy. "No, there's no mistake. You are my choice. No one comes to the Rope of the Dead of their own accord. You must be brought. I sent you to the Jungle of the South to see if you were strong enough to survive the ordeals you would have to face following the Rope of the Dead. I saw that you could. You'll learn. You're good at that."

This was the first time *Desheto* called me *Ani*, and from that time on he always referred to me as his scribe *Ani*. He went on, "To be my scribe you must grasp the Rope of the Dead, for only through the Rope will you ever understand my meaning."

Although I was afraid to ask the obvious question, I knew I needed to exert my will or be trampled by his wild fury, so I spoke as sincerely as I could. "What's in it for me? I mean, you're asking a lot of me. Don't I deserve something in return?"

After a long pause the Prince of Plants spoke, "There are few living people who know the world that I have invited you into and before you are done, almost all of them will be gone. What more does the Prince of Plants have to give you than access to his realm? Now, light the candle."

I fumbled around in the dark, searching for the box of matches and relit the candle. The flame of the beeswax slowly illuminated the dark room with the soft glow of its aura. But no matter how I tried, I could not raise my head to finally see what *Desheto* looked like. All I could see from the corner of my eye were the swirls of illuminated copal incense rising up from the clay burner on the altar and twisting into a woven rope.

Homing in on my insecurity, *Desheto* spoke with conviction. "This is the moment when you must choose. Walk away now and this will all become a distant dream. Or grab on to the Rope of the Dead and become my scribe *Ani*. Grab on to your destiny."

My hesitation ended and I grabbed the Rope of the Dead. It was like pulling the cord on a lamp in the dark, illuminating what was not visible before. The vaporous rope spun into a Vision Serpent that looked like a larger version of the Wind Serpents. When the Vision Serpent opened her mouth, the vibrant ghosts of naked *indios* with their bodies painted in intricate designs poured out, one by one, shimmering while they danced in and out of the shadows, as if moving between two realms.

As the ghosts danced, *Desheto* began to recite the mythical origin of the ritual.

SECTION 1
THE MYTH

CHAPTER 2
QUETZALCOATL, THE PLUMED SERPENT

The Plumed Serpent (Quetzalcoatl)

T he First World began as a fiery sun exploding from the Vision Serpent's mouth, an infinite black hole in the center of the Milky Way. After the rain extinguished this First World, the Mother and Father gods attempted three more times to create a lasting world. Failing each time, they passed the task on to their sons, the young Lord of the Wind, *Ehecatl,* and his brother, *Tezcatlipoca,* the Lord of Witches.

The brothers sought to surpass their parents by ensuring that the world they were creating would survive. The two young gods struggled to come up with a plan, each wanting to have his own way. The brothers' struggle soon escalated into an epic battle.

Wanting to stop the rivalry between her sons, the Elder Goddess sent her daughter, the Moon Goddess, *Coyolxauhqui,* to reason with her brothers. At the peak of their celestial battle, a speck of intergalactic dust floated down through the stars and caught the attention of the Moon Goddess and her dueling brothers. The Moon Goddess recognized this seemingly insignificant particle as the seed of the Fruit of Knowledge and told her brothers, "The tree that grows from this tiniest of seeds produces a fruit that can give us the knowledge we need to preserve the world."

Ignoring their sister's plea to bring balance between them, the brothers continued to fight, blinded by desire, both wishing to obtain the seed for themselves. *Ehecatl,* the Lord of the Wind, wanted the Fruit of Knowledge for the people he hoped to create. He believed it would give them the knowledge they would need to sustain the Fifth World. But the Lord of Witches, *Tezcatlipoca,* wanted to keep this sacred fruit only for the gods, feeling that humans would be more trouble than they were worth and that they would use the knowledge of the sacred fruit for destruction.

The young Lord of the Wind prevailed in this heavenly battle by sucking the tiny spore into his lungs. When *Tezcatlipoca,* the Lord of Witches, attempted to retrieve the seed from his brother, he stumbled and lost his balance, falling from the heavens. As he fell, he appeared as a blazing comet crashing into the churning primordial sea off the coast of what is today called the Yucatán peninsula in Mexico.

Startled by the explosion of the impact, the crocodile-billed Earth Monster, who lived beneath the sea, rose up from the ocean's depths and bit off the Lord of Witches' foot. The foot of the god poisoned the monster and as she died, the Lord of the Wind blessed the Earth Monster and transformed her into Mother Nature, the body of the Earth Mother: *Coatlicue*. The Lord of Witches' foot continued to ferment in the Earth Mother's belly and ultimately became the root of the subterranean Tree of Life.

This great tree spread its roots out through the Earth Mother's body and from these roots, the first plants sprouted. These plants lived and died, decaying into mud and clay, and from that clay, animals were formed and grew. These animals thrived in the fertile climate until the tiniest of life forms became the giant dinosaurs.

When the falling *Tezcatlipoca*, the Lord of Witches, splashed into the ocean, his blazing trail heated up the waters and changed the climate. Incubated by the heat, new bacteria grew and in other places ice formed where there once was sun. It was then that the giants who walked the earth went through a profound transformation. As the giants' offspring shrank in size, their fluffy down became plumage, which turned to feathers and then to wings. These creatures took flight, and from this group of flying serpents came one who was like no other, one who would one day be known as the Plumed Serpent.

The Lord of the Wind watched this transformation from his celestial home and was inspired by the Plumed Serpent. As he followed the Plumed Serpent's movements, *Ehecatl*, the Lord of the Wind, felt the seed of the Fruit of Knowledge stirring inside him. It whispered to him that he too would need to die and be transformed in order to create.

"Death is the greatest transformation and only through death will you be able to leave your beloved sky and enter the womb of the Earth Mother where the secret you seek is hidden," said the voice of the Fruit of Knowledge to the young Lord of the Wind.

To begin his death dance, the Lord of the Wind performed a ritual at that moment of silence between sunset and dusk when the animals of day go to sleep and those of night awaken. At this time of evening, the black hole in the middle of the Milky Way, the mouth at the throat of the Celestial Vision Serpent opens wide, waiting in anticipation to once again taste the spicy heat of the sun.

Afraid of missing the opportunity of this moment, the Lord of the Wind prayed to his parents, the Elder Gods, to send him a spirit guide. When the Ferryman of the Sun, the dog-faced god *Xolotl*, heard the Lord of the Wind's prayer, he realized that he had been chosen and he shot four lightning arrows towards the north, east, south and west.

The dog god then shot a fifth lightning bolt right through the young Lord of the Wind's heart to help him achieve the ultimate sacrifice of death. With his last breath, the Lord of the Wind blew the smoke of burning sweet grass outwards toward the places where the four arrows had landed, and in this way, he created the four directions. Each direction represented the birthplace of the four previous worlds that had been before the fifth and current world was created.

Having completed this act of self-sacrifice, the Lord of the Wind, now a ghost, followed the trail of the lightning bolt back towards Venus, the Evening Star. When he arrived, he petitioned *Xolotl*, the dog god who had shot the arrow through his heart, to guide him into the underworld, which was the only place where the Lord of the Wind could create humans.

Although every evening the dog-faced god had guided the sun into the underworld, he had never before led the wind. Gathering his courage, the dog god embraced this new challenge and bravely led the ghost of the Lord of the Wind across the Milky Way through the Pleiades and towards the constellation Sagittarius.

Here, the black hole of the Celestial Vision Serpent's open mouth reflected like a smoky, obsidian mirror and the young Lord of the Wind gazed upon his ghostly reflection in this tool of illusion, rapidly growing overcome with self-doubt. As his balance began to slip and the darkness around him sucked him down, the Lord of the Wind fell, his loyal companion at his side, tumbling in a sinking spiral through the Vision Serpent's throat, through the black hole at the center of the galaxy.

The pair of gods descended down through an endless night until a Wind of a Thousand Knives began to blow, piercing the skin of both the Lord of the Wind and *Xolotl*, ripping the flesh from their bones. Throughout their shared ordeal, the dog-faced god never left the Lord of the Wind and eventually guided him towards their destination: the center of the Black Flower of the Dead. Ever since this heroic journey, dogs have been known as "man's best friend."

When the underworld travelers reached the Black Flower of the Dead, the ghost of the Lord of the Wind stood before *Mictlantecuhtli*, the Lord of the Dead, and his skeletal wife, the Lady of the Dead, *Mictecacihuatl*. The Lord of the Wind bowed to these great ghosts, asking for the knowledge he needed to populate the Fifth World. The Lord of the Dead replied that his wife was the only one to possess this wisdom, so the Lord of the Wind turned toward the Lady of the Dead and caressed her with a gentle breeze. She had never before felt the sensation of the wind and was tantalized. Intrigued by the young god, she decided to help him with his quest.

"To make humans, the seed of a god must be mixed with the bones of the Grateful Dead," she explained.

"And who are the Grateful Dead, Mistress of the Black Flower?" the young ghost god asked with a graceful bow.

"They are the giant two-legged, ape-like creatures that roam across the land. Their bones become sacred upon death and so they are called the Grateful Dead."

The Lord of the Dead became jealous of the Lord of the Wind's flirtation with his wife. To make him appear foolish and less desirable, the Lord of the Dead gave the ghost of the wind god a very difficult task in return for his permission to visit the resting place of the sacred bones: the wind god was to make music with a conch shell from the sea to prove that he was also a god.

Aided by the wit and creativity that came from consuming the seed of the Fruit of Knowledge, the ghost of the wind god convinced a lowly worm of the underworld to bore a hole for a mouthpiece in the shell. To create sound, the young ghost god filled the conch with the ghosts of the buzzing bees he had found in the Black Flower. At this time, bees did not yet exist in the world of the living, nor did flowers. As the Lord of the Wind blew through the hole in the conch shell, the bees buzzed an eerie melody that won the heart of the Lady of the Dead. Ever since this time, the conch shell has been used as the Trumpet of the Dead and bees have been known as the Keepers of Flowers.

Although the Lady of the Dead was pleased by the young ghost god's success, her husband, the Lord of the Dead, was not. Jealous of the young ghost god's triumph, he decided to punish the Lord of the Wind with a nearly impossible task, one far more difficult than the first. Before mixing his seed with the bones of the Grateful Dead, the Lord of the Wind would have to face the Terrible Ordeals of the Nine Gods of Night. Only then would he have the wisdom needed to meet his destiny and create humans.

Sentenced by fate to suffer through the doubts of self-discovery, the ghost of the Lord of the Wind with his faithful guide dog wandered through the long night of the underworld. Ever onward they traveled, beyond the place in the Black Flower where the souls of animals were kept, searching for the bones of the Grateful Dead.

Over the course of their journey, the Lord of the Wind triumphed over more challenges in his grail search. These ordeals had become the steps of a ritual that were transforming him from what he was into what he could be. As he, *Ehecatl*, the Lord of the Wind, faced his fears, these ordeals became the stones upon which he sharpened his edge.

The dog-faced god eventually led his master to the pistil of the Black Flower where the sacred bones of the Grateful Dead were guarded by a gigantic, hibernating female toad, *Tlazolteotl*, a manifestation of the goddess of witches.

The Lord of the Dead had grown angrier and angrier as he watched the Lord of the Wind survive the challenges he had set for him. In an attempt to thwart him, the Lord of the Dead petitioned the Lord of Witches, *Tezcatlipoca*, to create an earthquake in the underworld to awaken the great toad goddess who guarded the sacred bones. But with great speed and stealth, the young Lord of the Wind, with his trusted companion, was able to sneak past this sleeping guard and carefully collect the bones of the Grateful Dead.

Still determined to stop them, the Lord of the Dead called upon the aid of *Tezcatlipoca* once again, and together they collaborated on a new plan to prevent the Lord of the Wind from creating humans. The Lord of Witches used his magic to send a covey of quail to intercept the young god as he continued on his journey. As the quail scattered in the darkness, the speckles on their feathers appeared as stars twinkling upon their wings and this startled the Lord of the Wind with memories of his beloved night sky. Momentarily homesick, he lost his balance and fell into a pit that the Lord of the Dead had dug to trap him. From his fall, many of the sacred bones collected by him became broken.

Even though his beloved guide dog stood guard watching over him in the dark pit, the Lord of the Wind felt alone. Here in the hopeless Ninth Ordeal of the quest, he mourned the breaking of the sacred bones and could not understand what could be learned from such a futile episode. In this moment of deep despair, his loyal companion lifted an ear to an approaching buzzing sound. The sound marked the arrival of the bees that had brought music to the conch shell. The bees dropped the wax of their hive into the pit where the wind god was trapped.

In the pit, the Lord of the Wind found a single shard of flint that had been chipped off the wall. He struck it against the stone floor, lighting the beeswax and so began the first ritual of the *velada*, the sacred candle ceremony. As he gazed into the crest of the flame of his fire, he heard an ancient voice speak.

"I am *Huehueteotl*, Grandfather Fire. I dwell in the crest of the flame."

The Lord of the Wind studied the flame's crest and he questioned, "Spirit of the Flame, have you come to feed upon my weakness?"

"No, my son. I am your Grandfather, the light in your darkness and giver of warmth. I am the oldest of the gods and I will be Grandfather to humanity, which will be your childrens' children in generations to come. In times of happiness, my fire will burn in your children's hearts and when there is sorrow, I will be the hope to the hopeless as I am to you on this endless night."

In spite of the fire god's reassuring words, the Lord of the Wind was still trapped in the depth of the pit of the Ninth Hell. Gradually, deep in the silence of an endless night, the young Lord began to hear the sounds of a faint and growing rhythm. This was the heartbeat of the Earth Mother, the goddess *Coatlicue*, and she told the Lord of the Wind to perform the first sacrifice, offering his own blood and seed to her.

With an awl carved from one of the bones of the Grateful Dead, the Lord of the Wind pierced himself, bleeding out his blood and seed onto the stones covering the ground of the pit. From this fertile blood, the bat god, *Piquete-zina,* was born and he flew out of the pit to bite the goddess *Xochiquetzal* in a way that took her virginity. From *Xochiquetzal's* maiden cap the first flowers were born, flowers which in the beginning had no aroma. The magical act of the birth of flowers lifted the Lord of the Wind to his feet and caused him to dance on the broken bones of the Grateful Dead. As he danced, the Lord of the Wind noticed a matrix of delicate white roots in a magnificent pattern that permeated the dank roof of the underworld.

Grandfather Fire spoke to him again, "These are the roots of the Tree of Life and the tapestry of nature, the weave that binds together every living thing upon this land. Collect these fibers of the souls of plants and braid them into the Rope of the Dead, so that plants can always be the bridge of communication between you, the gods and the generations to come."

Continuing to dance, the Lord of the Wind began to collect the fibers of plant souls, the mycelia that are the roots of the Tree of Life. With these threads, he carefully wove a rope that hung down from the world of plants above into the underworld of the Black Flower below.

Through the Pool of Souls, the Lord of the Dead had been watching the fall of *Ehecatl*, the Lord of the Wind. By now, the Lord of the Dead no longer wished him harm. Instead, he had gained respect for the wind god and wished to end his pain. So out of the darkness and with the stealth of an owl, the Lord of the Dead followed the steps of the Lord of the Wind's grail journey down into the pit of the Ninth Hell. Instead of attacking the Lord of the Wind, the Lord of the Dead began to dance with him.

As they danced together back to back, the Lord of the Wind finally made his peace with Death. While the two gods, old and young, danced, the semen and blood that trickled from the Lord of the Wind's wounded penis mixed, and this fertile seed was sprinkled upon the bones of the Grateful Dead. This was the first Ghost Dance, and from this dance, human souls appeared in the Americas and rose up as butterflies, bees and hummingbirds before taking human form.

With his quest now embraced by the Lord of the Dead, the Lord of the Wind climbed the rope woven from the souls of plants out of the Pit of Hopelessness and as he emerged, the ordeals of the Ninth Hell of the long night ended. At that moment, the bees pollinated one of the fungal flowers that grew from the goddess *Xochiquetzal's* flesh, and fragrance in the floral kingdom was born.

Led by the sound of the Earth Mother's beating heart, he finally arrived at her altar. The Earth Mother *Coatlicue* was woven together with rattlesnakes and had a double serpentine head. She was the Keeper of the Paradises that lay just beyond the pit of the Ninth Hell. When the Lord of the Wind reached the Earth Mother, she sacrificed him upon her altar so that he might have form in the world of the living.

With an obsidian knife, the Earth Mother cut his heart out from his ghostly body and captured the aura of effervescence around the still-beating organ. His essence she ground together with his bones and placed this concoction into a conch shell and blew. With her sacred breath, *Coatlicue* brought back to life the ghost of the son who had once blessed and helped create her.

The Lord of the Wind's spirit rose out of the conch shell in a vaporous swirl and drifted up through the Vision Serpent's celestial throat. As her mouth opened, out flew a spectacular feathered serpent and with this creation, the cycle of transformations was finally complete.

Ehecatl, the young Lord of the Wind, had become *Quetzalcoatl*, the Plumed Serpent. The Plumed Serpent rose up and flew across the Milky Way. The thirteen hummingbirds, bees and butterflies that had followed him continued on into the world of the living and came to rest in the Americas, in the great *Tule* tree of Oaxaca, Mexico.

These winged creatures, born from the bones of the Grateful Dead and the seed of a god, were to become the souls of the first humans. Because the bones of the Grateful Dead had broken when the Lord of the Wind fell into the pit, people came into the world in all different sizes.

CHAPTER 3
THE GRAIL OF THE AMERICAS

Precious Flower (Xochiquetzal)

P erched in the heavens as Venus, a radiant Plumed Serpent
hovered, his feathered chest rising and falling as he filled his
lungs and stretched out his scaly neck, exhaling the seed of the
Fruit of Knowledge. With a burst of air, the wind carried the
seed down from the heavens and it came to rest in the cloud
forest of Mother Earth's Fertile Crescent. From this seed a

subterranean tree sprouted, and as it blossomed, the Fruit of Knowledge appeared.

This fruit was intended to be a means through which humans, their ancestors, plants and the gods could all communicate. By eating this sacred fruit, the ancestors could help their living descendants, humans, to maintain a respectful relationship with the gods of the elements of nature and all living things.

Tezcatlipoca, the Lord of Witches, watched his brother's children struggle in the darkness of his obsidian mirror. Gazing through the smoke, he looked far into the future and saw his beloved Mother Earth ravaged and polluted by these same people, the Two-Legged Ones the Plumed Serpent had created. Wanting to save Mother Earth, the Lord of Witches devised a plan to get rid of the troublesome Two-Legged Ones. With sleight of hand, he drew the smoke out of his mirror and wove it into a Veil of Illusion. Then he transformed himself into the Lord of Days, and with great stealth, he carefully cast his veil over the Plumed Serpent's dream of civilization. With his Veil of Illusion secure, *Tezcatlipoca* was providing humans with the exact tool they would need to destroy themselves in the future.

While the Plumed Serpent watched the drama unfold from the heavens above, his feathers bristled as he began to realize the obvious; his brother's Veil of Illusion would easily trick his naïve children. Even though they had tasted the Fruit of Knowledge, humans still did not possess the wisdom needed to interpret this knowledge correctly. So the Plumed Serpent decided to impart a ritual that would teach humans to interpret the wisdom of the Fruit of Knowledge. He called this ritual the Ghost Dance.

THE STRANGER

The Plumed Serpent chose a merchant sailor to carry the seed of the Fruit of Knowledge across the sacred Sea of Testes. This seaman traveled across the great ocean in search of the coca and tobacco leaves that the kings near the Fertile Crescent used in their burial ceremonies. The Stranger shipwrecked on a beach in what is now the Mexican state of Veracruz. When the Olmec people found him he was half dead. The only other survivor of the journey was the Stranger's constant companion, a hairless dog.

A beautiful Mixtec girl named *Xochiquetzal* or Precious Flower nursed the olive-skinned seaman back to health. The Stranger fell in love with the scent of Precious Flower before he ever opened his eyes, and Precious Flower's heart soon warmed to the mysterious, bearded man who had washed ashore.

Precious Flower was named well, as she knew the nature of plants and flowers as if they were her own. Plants knew how to communicate with her without using words. It was Precious Flower who showed the Stranger how to make offerings to the first god of the Mixtec, Grandfather Fire, and this god taught the couple how to grow their love.

"Love is the warmth of my fire," said Grandfather Fire. "Learn to nurture my flame from a spark, and by observing and learning the nature of fire, you will know how to nurture love in each other."

Over time, the bond of love between the Stranger and Precious Flower grew stronger and the Stranger became more and more Americanized, inheriting the attributes of the land through the soil, a soil made up of all those that had passed before him: animal, plant and mineral.

As the Stranger and Precious Flower's love grew, so did a challenge that threatened to separate them. Precious Flower was a prized concubine of the Lord of Witches' high priest, who had no intentions of allowing a lowly stranger to take her for his own. The star-crossed lovers could not bear to be torn apart and ran away together on a journey to Precious Flower's homeland, the Sierra Mazateca.

Upon arriving at their destination in the Mountains of the Clouds, Precious Flower found a small, pockmarked rock and told the Stranger that they should rest at that spot.

While Precious Flower slept, she dreamt that a large, red ant removed from the rock a corn kernel the color of the Indian people and took it back into his anthill. Her lover then became a black ant and snuck inside the red ant's *kiva* and stole the prized kernel. Then the black ant turned back into the Stranger, and Precious Flower awoke to find her lover holding the corn kernel in the palm of his hand.

The young seafarer was like the wind, a constantly moving catalyst who knew little of the land. Precious Flower stood as a great tree, growing steadily in the same place over time, completely aware of her surroundings. She was trained in the way of plants and knew that if placed in the ground, the kernel would grow.

Precious Flower nurtured this new life, while she instructed the Stranger to sacrifice a turkey to the god of thunder who, from then on, would always protect sacred crops. In honor of the thunder, the Stranger shook the first Ghost Dance rattle made of fifty-two tiny quartz stones sculpted by Mother Nature. Then he prayed to *Tloloc Sequah*, the god of rain, and *Tloloc* answered the Stranger's prayers with the rain. Soon, the corn planted by Precious Flower and the Stranger grew and one corn stalk eventually became many.

Precious Flower picked the kernels from the largest cobs to replant and with each planting the kernels became larger and larger.

To win her freedom, Precious Flower and the Stranger brought these kernels of the sun back to the semi-nomadic Olmec as tribute, and they in turn planted them. Precious Flower and the Stranger won their freedom when the Olmec harvested the first crop of corn. With this first crop, the tribes became sedentary and a civilization was born.

The Stranger was an outsider and not part of any tribe. Because of this, he was able to avoid the endless feuds of the people and move amongst them unharmed. As he grew older and wiser, the Stranger became one of the elders of his adopted people and wanted to help their newborn civilization survive. He watched the interplay between nature and their crops, and he realized that their dream of civilization could only survive through maintaining a communication and respect with the gods of the elements of nature. Nomadic people can just move away if the weather turns bad. The survival of civilization depends on the weather needed to grow the crops in that one place.

On a vision quest to commune with the gods of the elements of nature, Precious Flower and the now-elderly Stranger returned one last time to the Sierra Mazateca. This was the sacred mountain where the two lovers had found the first kernel of corn. As the Stranger and Precious Flower slowly climbed the high mountains toward the clouds, a distant wind began to rustle the leaves on the trees and the old man could hear the voice of the wind. The wind rushed towards them and lifted the old couple in step with each other, carrying them up the mountain until they reached the top of the clouds. Thunder rumbled and lightning cracked as they entered the realm of the Seven Sacred Caves within the Crucible of the Summer Storm.

Precious Flower now performed the second *velada* ceremony. Placing marigold flowers on an altar, she lit a single beeswax candle and ignited copal incense to release sacred smoke. Precious Flower then consumed the sacred leaves of the square-stemmed sage plant the Olmec used to commune with their gods. She spoke to the flame, saying, "Grandfather Fire, I am your daughter, a Clean Sister."

As she sang in splendid tones, the smoke rose, following the punctuation in her voice, and the old Stranger began to dance. He ghost danced to the beat of the pulse of the Americas, as the intervals of his lover's voice flowed gracefully before the flame of Grandfather Fire. As the Stranger danced like the god *Quetzalcoatl*, he also bled blood and semen. Within his essence was the seed of the Fruit of Knowledge that the Stranger had carried from the land of the Fertile Crescent.

Having bled out the last of his life force, the tired, old man could dance no more and let go of his earthly bonds. He lay upon the Earth Mother's breast with her heartbeat giving him shelter from the approaching storm, and the wind howled with untamed fury and ripped through the cloud forest, racing towards the scent of death.

Riding the crest of the wind was the wild and free Spirit of the Americas, an apparition of the Plumed Serpent which flapped its wings as it circled around the old man. The frogs began to sing and the wind that the Plumed Serpent rode in upon brought the clouds and with them, the rain. Through the second Ghost Dance, the Stranger had made an agreement with the gods of the elements of nature to help Precious Flower's budding civilization. Lightning hit the old man's footprints and then, like the Pietà, the Mother Earth took back the remains of her precious son. By inhaling the totem of the Americas with his final breath, the old

Stranger had become one with the Plumed Serpent and completed that cycle of the Ghost Dance.

CHAPTER 4
THE LITTLE ONES

The Tree of the Fruit of Knowledge

P recious Flower was amazed to see the Little Ones, the
sacred mushrooms that were the Fruit of Knowledge,
springing forth from the ground where her husband had spilled
his blood and semen. As she bent down to pick the fruit of her
husband's seed, a viper snake crawled out between the sacred
mushrooms and spoke to Precious Flower.

"Eat of these Little Ones, grown from the seed of the Fruit of Knowledge, and you will dance with your true love again."

So just before dusk Precious Flower lit a candle and ate the Little Ones, curling up in a fetal position as the mushrooms took hold. Through the crest of the candle's flame, the head of an old, bearded man appeared, with his beard forming the flame and his voice as soothing as only an old man's can be.

"I am your Grandfather *Huehueteotl*. Do not fear me. I am the warmth on a cold night and that which heats the food you eat. My child, I have come to give you a divine gift, the means to ensure the survival of your future generations: the map to the steps of the Ghost Dance. These are the steps needed to commune with the gods of the elements of nature who manifest the weather. But before you can receive this sacred gift you must ceremonially collect for me the fibers of the souls of plants. Weave them together into a rope that will join humans and plants, and through the plants you will once again be able to commune with your husband."

Shimmering in the illuminated smoke of the copal were wispy twirls of fine luminescent fibers. Precious Flower began to reach through the smoke towards the fibers, but the shimmering strands dispersed at her touch.

"How do you weave strands of smoke together, Grandfather?"

"Very carefully," Grandfather Fire replied.

After many frustrating attempts, Precious Flower's touch became so delicate she could pull the luminous plant fibers from the smoke without disturbing them. Once she had these vaporous strands of plant souls gathered, she wove them carefully together until she had a thick rope in her hands. As Precious Flower held on to this rope of smoke, the ground suddenly gave way and she tumbled backwards, falling into what appeared to be the long dark throat of the Vision Serpent. Precious Flower's heart raced, and panicking, she let go of the rope, her only connection to the world of the living. As she fell, Precious Flower heard the Grandfather's voice saying, "Grab the rope, granddaughter!"

Without thought, Precious Flower grabbed the Rope of the Dead, and as she did, the world of reality she was accustomed to exploded into chaos. Within the chaos were heard a profound heartbeat and the calming voice of the Elder Goddess.

"A man must spiritually die to be reborn a Ghost Dancer, while a woman awakens from a dream, like a flower at dawn, to become a Clean Sister."

Precious Flower wondered what this meant and the Mother god explained. "I sent my daughter, the Moon Goddess, to bring balance to a world created by her warring brothers. Now I pass on a lineage to you to create a sisterhood that will protect the Ghost Dance and its dancers until the completion of the ritual."

Opening her eyes, Precious Flower realized that she was no longer falling, but instead floating over a fabulous crystalline kaleidoscope of mosaic architecture. Just below this awe-inspiring vision was the underworld of the Black Flower where the dead reside and the place where she would once again see her true love. There, wandering through the dank canyons of this underworld, was the skeletal ghost of her beloved husband.

At that moment, she realized that the steps of the grail he followed were a reflection of the living journey the Olmec people had embarked upon in the world of the living. With this awakening, Precious Flower left the dream world of the Black Flower. Her return to consciousness made her aware that the Little Ones were not only a means for her to continue dancing with her own true love, but they were also a sacrament for the Olmec to commune with the gods of the elements of nature. Through the Little Ones, the Olmec would now be able to maintain a relationship with the weather and in this way continue to give birth to civilization by growing corn.

Every year when the rains came, Precious Flower returned to the forest where her husband had died to perform her *velada*. After lighting her beeswax candle and eating the Little Ones, she would once again journey to the Black Flower to seek out the ghost of her true love in the Crucible of the Summer Storm.

Year after year, Grandfather Fire and the mysterious voices behind the Little Ones taught her the steps to the ghost ritual, until Precious Flower was able to dance with the ghost of her beloved. And one by one, the ancestors brought other special women to the mountain. From these women, Precious Flower formed a Mazatec sisterhood of healers. They were called the *Comadres Limpiadas*. This sisterhood was based on the balance of health and cleanliness.

Every year when the Little Ones came out of hiding, Precious Flower instructed her Clean Sisters in the art of communicating with their ancestors by ingesting the mushrooms. This was done to continue the Ghost Dance ritual until its future completion and thereby maintain the human niche in the weave of nature. This practice became known as The Prophecy of Seven Generations and was based on the Mixtec belief that the sacred number seven represented the continuity of generations.

Precious Flower spoke to her Clean Sisters of the prophecy. "A time will come when we as a people will also have to take the journey through the underworld. This will happen when we turn on our Mother, and the Clean Sisters and the Ghost Dancers will have to bring back a dying Tree of Life. You, my sisters, will preserve the ritual until that day comes."

Precious Flower continued, "Now, bring me masons to build a temple where scribes will record in codices the steps of my husband's Ghost Dance."

And so it was that a great Sky Temple was built near the mountain peak of Chilchotla and the best scribes were brought to illustrate pictographs of the Ghost Dance in a codex. The pre-Columbian illustration of the Plumed Serpent ghost dancing back to back with the ghostly Lord of the Dead in the Codex Borgia would survive across time. However, it would not be recognized as the actual Ghost Dance until a scribe revealed its secret meaning at the end of the greater Ghost Dance cycle. Only then could the ritual that had begun before the time of the Toltec finally be completed.

When her task was finished, Precious Flower left the world of the living to join her beloved husband in the Black Flower below. Her last words for her Little Sisters were, "Women do not die like men to be born again; they awaken to awareness from a great sleep like a morning glory flower unfolding at dawn's first light."

When a Clean Sister dies, the Mother cries for her special child and it rains for seven days.

As the molten earth swallowed Precious Flower, she entered the Black Flower of Death and awakened from her great sleep to begin her own grail journey through the underworld. Precious Flower arrived in the paradise of the Fifth Petal and found her true love. Together as ghosts, they embraced and danced.

Since then, each year, on the right day and at the time when the great Vision Serpent of the Milky Way opens its mouth the widest, the Clean Sisters could eat the Little Ones and dance with the ghosts of their own true love.

CHAPTER 5
THE TOLTEC GHOST DANCER

The separation of the soul and spirit from the astral body

T hrough the Plumed Serpent and Precious Flower's gift of
corn, the Olmec and Mixtec cultures merged together and
became the Toltec. In the name of Precious Flower's true love,
the Plumed Serpent, the arts, healing and fair trade flourished for
a thousand years of harmony in the great valley of Mexico. Much

of this fortune came as a blessing from the gods in the form of favorable weather and well-defined seasons.

But the Lord of Witches, *Tezcatlipoca*, was disgusted by the success of the Toltec civilization, viewing them as parasites who would eventually consume his beloved Earth Mother. To lead them astray, The Lord of Witches cast his Veil of Illusion over the Toltec. The illusion convinced the Toltec rulers and priests that they should build shrines to solidify their relationship with *Quetzalcoatl*, the Plumed Serpent. Ironically, the more the Toltec tried to capture their tribal totem in stone, the further away the elusive spirit flew.

The Toltec lords did not realize that the pyramids, holy cities and monuments they were building to honor their god, the Plumed Serpent, were severing their delicate ties to the Tree of Life. Without those ties, what was once sacred grew shallow and the moment became ripe for even greater deception.

From the shadows of a dank temple chamber on top of the Pyramid of the Plumed Serpent, *Tezcatlipoca*, dressed as the Lord of Days, watched the Toltec seal their fate. But the god was caught in a predicament. In order to destroy humanity, the Lord of Days would first have to allow the Toltec to hurt what he loved most: Mother Earth.

The destruction of the roots of the Tree of Life brought on a drought that was followed by a pestilence of locust and famine. Not recognizing their mistake, the Toltec felt betrayed by their god, *Quetzalcoatl*, and in their ignorance they turned back to the god that they worshipped before their Thousand Years of Peace: *Tezcatlipoca*. For the first time in a thousand years, the priests built a pyramid in honor of *Tezcatlipoca* and resumed the practice of human sacrifice. After eighteen years, the rains finally came and the Toltec rejoiced, proudly calling themselves the slaves of the Lord of Days.

Only the Clean Sisterhood understood the profound mistake that the Toltec had made. *Desheto* had warned the sisters that *Tezcatlipoca*, the Toltecs' new lord and master, planned to sacrifice their entire civilization in order to save Mother Nature. To stop the wrath of *Tezcatlipoca* and ensure the survival of the humans' niche in nature, the Clean Sisterhood called upon the Ghost Dancers to once again begin their ritual.

Thirteen Toltec Ghost Dance initiates were chosen and led to the bottom of the Pyramid of the Plumed Serpent where they walked counterclockwise around the Path of the Dead at the religious center of Teotihuacan. At that moment before dusk, a Clean Sister arrived from the Mountains of the Clouds with the Little Ones wrapped in leaves and performed a *velada* ceremony. Bathing the Little Ones in copal smoke, an elder sister offered three pairs each to the thirteen Toltec initiates, and instructed them, "Eat the Little Ones in pairs so their journey to the dead won't be lonely."

After the Toltec initiates ate the Little Ones, they lined up and each placed their left hand on the shoulder of the one in front of them. Then a huge Plumed Serpent puppet was placed over all thirteen initiates' heads. The puppet was constructed of woven fabric and wood, and the crest of its plumed head was fashioned out of emerald-green *Quetzal* bird feathers. As the Ghost Dance initiates entered a world of darkness inside the puppet, a log drum began to play. In step with the rhythm, the Ghost Dance initiates snaked their way up the pyramid.

In the dark, smoke-filled temple above, *Tezcatlipoca* and his priests chanted, preparing themselves for the arrival of the Ghost Dance initiates that the Lord of Days planned to destroy. As they climbed the steps, the earth's shadow began to eclipse the moon.

When the Plumed Serpent puppet reached the temple on top of the pyramid, it stopped in front of an incense burner from which smoke rose and twisted into the Rope of the Dead. *Tezcatlipoca's* priests sat on each side of the chamber chanting, and against the back wall stood *Tezcatlipoca's* Black Mirror of Illusion. As the priests chanted, the initiates inside the Plumed Serpent puppet felt as if the priest's words were sucking them through the surface of this Black Mirror and they grabbed on to the smoky Rope of the Dead.

Seizing the moment, *Tezcatlipoca* manifested as the Lord of Witches, and with an obsidian knife, he cut the rope just above the last initiate. With no rope to hold on to, the thirteenth Toltec Ghost Dancer fell down the Vision Serpent's throat, his flesh torn from his body by a wind of knives. When he hit the bottom of the pit, the now-skeletal Ghost Dancer picked himself up, determined to reweave the severed Rope of the Dead, the only means to escape the underworld and save his tribe.

Inside the chamber of the pyramid, *Tezcatlipoca* had disappeared and his remaining priests trembled with fear. By cutting the Rope of the Dead, the living Toltec would no longer be able to communicate with their ancestors, but neither could *Tezcatlipoca's* priests. These priests had been double-crossed by their own lord and without the rope, there was nothing to ensure that future rituals would be performed correctly.

The Toltecs' fall from grace was only interrupted once, many centuries later, when the One Reed cycle of their calendar began anew. During this cycle, a Toltec king named Topiltzin ascended the throne, claiming to be a human incarnation of the Plumed Serpent, *Quetzalcoatl*. The king attempted to restore the Golden Age of the Toltecs' thousand years of peace, but was subsequently tricked by *Tezcatlipoca's* priests with sex, drugs and the Mirror of Vanity. Driven out of the city of Tula in disgrace, this self-proclaimed incarnation of the Toltec god fled to the eastern sea, sailing away on a raft of serpents with the sign of the four winds upon its sail.

But before leaving, the dethroned king falsely foretold of *Quetzalcoatl's* return in the cyclical year of One Reed. The date for the fulfillment of Topiltzin's twisted prediction was the European calendar year of 1519.

SECTION 2
THE UNTOLD HISTORY

CHAPTER 6
THE LADY OF THE DEAD

The Clean Sisterhood

T he Toltec Ghost Dancer who had fallen when *Tezcatlipoca* cut the Rope of the Dead now stood before the Lord and Lady of the Dead, as the Plumed Serpent had once done before him. To mend the Rope of the Dead, he too would have to face the Nine Ordeals and Thirteen Awakenings of the Black Flower by following the footprints of his patron on a quest through the Americas.

While the Ghost Dancer began his journey with his guide dog *Xolotl* at his side, a new goddess forced her way into the Black Flower. Those who knew her called her the Mother of All Plagues.

The Mother of All Plagues was a blind goddess who ruled over civilization, deciding who lived and who died, who vanished and who thrived. *Tezcatlipoca* was convinced that disease was the way to finally rid his beloved Mother Earth of her human parasites, so he petitioned the Mother of All Plagues to awaken her minions and come to the Americas.

Hidden behind a rotting petal in what was once a paradise, the fallen Toltec Ghost Dancer watched as the Plague Mother filled her lungs and blew a breath of life into the tangle of thousands of tiny translucent worms that lay dormant in the petal's rotting folds as they waited to be born again. Her foul breath was called the *xawara*. As the Plague Mother blew, these white worms came out of hibernation, writhing and crawling over each other. And she brought them to the Americas on the ships of the first Europeans.

THE AZTEC

On Good Friday, March 5th, 1519, their hair drenched in blood, the soothsayers of the Aztec capital city of Tenochtitlan made human sacrifices to their god of the sun, *Tonatiuh*. Unlike most conquerors, the Aztec gave up their own gods and adopted the defeated Toltecs' mythology. As the new lords of Mesoamerica, they feared the Toltecs' ancient prediction of a coming eclipse.

For many days the Aztec priests had fed the sun god his favorite offering, the effervescent life force which was contained in the aura surrounding a still-beating human heart. But no matter how they tried, the Aztec priests could not stop the moon from blocking the sun out of the sky.

Cowering in the dark shadow of the moon, the Aztecs were relieved when the sun reappeared once again. At that same moment, the conquistador Hernán Cortés' ship appeared like a vision along the tropical shoreline of what is now Veracruz, Mexico.

Word was sent to the Aztec capital, Tenochtitlan, that the eclipse had manifested a vision upon the sea. This stirred a profound paranoia among the Aztec oligarchy, who were afraid that the returning Toltec god, the Plumed Serpent, would punish them for breaking his law banning human sacrifice.

Inside the Aztec king's palace, the nervous priests bickered amongst themselves, unable to agree on whether this was the returning *Quetzalcoatl* or a false prophet. They sought counsel from the goddess *Coatlicue* who told them to consult a sacred talking stone. The stone warned the Aztec that *Quetzalcoatl* had returned to destroy them for their evil ways and so King Montezuma offered golden gifts in an attempt to peacefully stop the scurvy-ridden *conquistadores* from reaching his urban center of Tenochtitlan.

Insisting on a personal meeting with the god-king Montezuma, the Spaniards persisted and arrived at the capital. Once there, Cortés was so awed by the golden splendor of the city, he dropped his god-like façade. Letting greed overtake his common sense, Cortés kidnapped Montezuma and held him for a gold ransom. After experiencing the greed of his captors, Montezuma realized that Cortés was a mere mortal and not the returning god *Quetzalcoatl*. Then, with newfound confidence, the king secretly ordered his eagle and jaguar warriors to drive the *conquistadores* from the capital. Although most of the conquistadors were killed during this Night of Sorrow, a few made it back to Veracruz with the aid of the Tlaxcalan enemies of the Aztec.

After three long-embattled years in the swamp, reinforcements and slaves arrived from the Spanish Colony of Cuba carrying diseases like cholera and smallpox. Messengers infected with disease were then sent to the unsuspecting Aztecs' capital city. This arrival of the Mother of All Plagues proved to be a painful yet decisive change of events in the battle for the conquest of Mesoamerica.

During the rainy season of the summer of 1521, the *conquistadores* once again marched towards the Aztec capital of Tenochtitlan. Walking alongside Cortés' horse was a slave girl whom he had captured and baptized, naming her Doña Marina. Doña Marina had quickly learned the Spanish language and it soon became obvious that she nurtured a hunger for revenge towards her own people, who had sold her into slavery. As Cortés' confidante, she revealed to him the inherent weaknesses of the Aztec people and in so doing became Cortés' tool of conquest, as he would later become her weapon for revenge.

At the end of July, as the rains poured down, Doña Marina led the troops into a large pueblo named *Mictecacihuatlan* after the Lady of the Dead. As an attempt to appease Cortés, the Aztec authorities in the pueblo had invited him to witness their joyous *Miccailhuitontli*, or Lady of the Dead ceremony. The Aztec oligarchy appeared to be oblivious to the wake of destruction that had just arrived.

Dressed in their finest gold and cotton clothing, the upper classes prepared for one of their favorite holidays. *Miccailhiutontli* was the seasonal ceremony of the same Lady of the Dead who had helped the ghost of *Quetzalcoatl* retrieve the bones of the Grateful Dead. The Lady of the Dead ceremony was the Aztec re-interpretation of the Toltec Ghost Dance, with a major difference: while the Toltec Ghost Dancers communed with the totem of the people, the Plumed Serpent, the Aztec Lady of the Dead participants communed with the ghosts of their own loved ones.

The pageantry of the Aztec ritual began when the Clean Sisterhood arrived from the land of the most ancient gods, the Mountains of the Clouds. To the beat of wooden drums and flutes, the Sisters walked counterclockwise around the Pathway of the Dead towards the Temple of Quetzalcoatl. The Aztec valued the Clean Sisterhood because the Clean Sisters were the last remaining direct link to the origin of Toltec/Mixtec mysticism. For this reason, the Mazatec Clean Sisterhood was protected by the Aztec state and could travel safely throughout the kingdom.

Stopping at the foot of the Pyramid of the Plumed Serpent, the Clean Sisters began their ascent, walking past giant heads of plumed dragons carved from stone and entering the mouth of the temple. Inside the first chamber, yellow and orange *cempoalxochitl*, the sacred marigold flowers, adorned the altar of the Lady of the Dead. The Aztec priests had their faces painted red and black, while the Clean Sisters wore their best white *huipil* tunics, delicately woven with images of magical flowers and hummingbirds.

Dressed in armor and wearing his plumed helmet, Cortés and his friars followed the Clean Sisters up the steps of the pyramid. Children wearing butterfly, bee and hummingbird costumes danced around Cortés, offering him hot chocolate laced with mushrooms to drink, but offended by the heathen ritual, he refused.

At dusk, the ceremony of the Lady of the Dead officially began with the blowing of the conch shell. The conch shell's eerie drone punctuated that moment between the time the animals of day went to sleep and those of night awakened.

With a delicate humility, a Clean Sister approached the altar and lit a single flame, and then together the Sisters said, "We are Morning Star Women, we are the Keepers of the Ghost Dance, we are the Clean Sisters."

A Clean Sister lit copal incense in a brazier made in the form of the bearded and double-crowned god of fire. Streams of twisting smoke rose and the Clean Sister used that smoke to purify the *Teonanacatl*, the Little Ones known as the Astonishing Gift of the Gods.

Then the Aztecs ate their *Teonanacatl* with clear honey of the little black bee mixed with hot chocolate and lay down to rest on straw mats. As they rested, the Clean Sisters chanted to Grandfather Fire, "Grandfather, please call upon the Lady of the Dead to graciously open the door to her realm, the mouth of the great Vision Serpent." The first Clean Sister then extinguished the single flame with the belled top of an orchid, and in complete darkness the sisters sang to the Vision Serpent, inviting him to appear.

When the right moment arrived, a Clean Sister relit the beeswax candle on the altar, transforming the wall drawings into animated visions, which played host to the billows of copal smoke that twisted into the form of a Vision Serpent.

Under the effect of the *Teonanacatl*, the Aztecs then rose from their mats while the Vision Serpent in the copal smoke opened its mouth. One by one, the full bodies of the ghosts of the beloved dead sprang forth from the Vision Serpent's mouth, billowing into the earthly dimension.

The Aztec greeted the ghosts of their relatives with joyous dance and song, while Cortés watched the spectacle in disdain. Having not partaken in the sacrament-laced chocolate, he saw no ghosts and his Catholic morality was appalled by the Aztecs' joyous behavior towards death.

"Only the Holy Ghost is considered sacred, and all other ghosts are nothing more than evil minions of the devil," Cortés' friars declared.

Cortés was certain that the New World was a dark realm of the devil, where satanic ceremonies were performed under giant statues of plumed, beast-like dragons. Just like the European grail legend, this dragon also guarded a great treasure. For Cortés, who saw himself as a latter-day crusading knight, this New World was becoming a living hell, with the Plumed Serpent its presiding apocalyptic beast.

From then on, Cortés metaphorically and literally drew his sword to stop the Lady of the Dead ceremony. In a frenzy of horror, Toledo steel chopped off the arms and heads of the intoxicated and joyous dancers. The educated *padres* did nothing to stop the butchery, realizing that the Aztec relationship with their ancestral ghosts was the key to this heathen people's uniqueness and resistance to evangelization. But even with these barbaric tactics, the conquistadors could not completely crush the Lady of the Dead ceremony.

When the Aztec priests in Tenochtitlan found out about the massacre at the Lady of the Dead ceremony, they began to make hundreds of human sacrifices to appease their angry god, *Huitzilopochtli.*

"We bring you food, an offering of the essence of life force. Oh great Lord of our ancestors, we sacrifice so you may punish the invaders that have insulted you," intoned the priests to their god.

The Aztecs made tributes of life force in the form of blood, and though the sacrifices were plentiful, *Huitzilopochtli*, known as the Hummingbird of the South, was still not appeased and the Aztec began to lose their fight against Cortés. The losses were mainly due to the aid of Cortés' new allies, the Aztecs' sworn enemies, the Tlaxcalans, whom Doña Marina had convinced to support the *conquistadores*.

When the Aztec found out what their slave had done, they renamed her Malinche, the "Tongue That Sticks a Knife in Your Back." With the aid of the Tlaxcalans, the conquistadors were able to reach the Aztecs' capital city of Tenochtitlan, but this time the invaders had a secret weapon far more powerful than guns and steel.

Entering the city, the *conquistadores* were overpowered by the stench of rotting corpses. Cortés' couriers had infected the urban Aztec with terrible diseases including typhus, cholera and smallpox, which had arrived from the slave colony of Cuba. The Mother of All Plagues had Tenochtitlan in a death grip, and the fearful Tlaxcalans refused to enter the city. Instead they surrounded the capital, not letting anyone out.

The *conquistadores,* on the other hand, had built up immunity by surviving the plagues of Europe. They believed that Christ, their One True God, would protect them from these evil vapors as they attacked the few eagle warriors who could still stand and fight. The diseases from the Old World, brought in from the slave colony of Cuba, accomplished what Cortés could not: the end of the era of the Aztec.

After this initial conquest, Montezuma was executed to prove to the Aztec that their king was not a god. Cortés was also emphatic about outlawing the Lady of the Dead Ghost Dance ceremony, which caused a major revolt since the Aztec were not willing to give up this important ritual. Concerned with Cortés' failure to put down the uprising, the Church in Europe came up with a weapon that proved to be far more effective than the sword in the campaign to spiritually conquer the Aztec: the calendar.

THE POWER OF THE CALENDAR

As the reign of Pope Leo X gave way to Pope Adrian and then Pope Clement VII, the papacy in Rome officially changed the date of the Lady of the Dead ceremony from June 18th to November 1st and 2nd. In this way, the new Pope merged the pagan ceremony together with the Catholic All Saints' and All Souls' Days. The holiday then became known as the *Día de Muertos* (or *Día de los Muertos*), the Day of the Dead.

By changing the date of the celebration, the original sacrament was removed from the ceremony because the Astonishing Gift of the Gods, the sacred mushroom sacrament of the Aztec Ghost Dance ceremony, only grew during the rainy season of June, July and August.

Thus, the Mexican Day of the Dead holiday became the living remnant of the Lady of the Dead ceremony, which itself was the Aztec re-interpretation of the Toltec Ghost Dance. Ultimately, it substituted the original sacrament of the Little Ones with alcohol.

When the Aztec Lady of the Dead ceremony was replaced by the Day of the Dead holiday, the entire relationship between the Mesoamericans' ancestral ghosts and their descendants was altered. This transition caused a chain of events, beginning with the Clean Sisters' loss of their position as the priestesses of the Lady of the Dead ceremony. Instead, Catholic nuns and priests imported from Europe took over as the spiritual authorities of the Day of the Dead ceremony.

Without the protection of the Aztec state, the Clean Sisters became fair game for both the newly arrived Spanish Inquisition and the Tlaxcalan witches who were still seeking revenge against the newly conquered Aztec. These witches were hungry to consume the vibrant life force of the oldest sisterhood in the Americas, the Clean Sisters, who were the keepers of the Ghost

Dance. Aztec and Tlaxcalan witches both sent their *naguals*, or animal spirits, into the dreams of the Clean Sisters, with the intention of consuming their souls and reaping their power. At the same time the Church smashed the sisterhood's sacred idols.

When the witch hunts began, Clean Sisters were brought before the Inquisition of the Church of New Spain. The *Comadres Limpiadas*, the Clean Sisterhood, became the first group of women the Inquisition tortured for witchcraft in the New World.

To escape further persecution, the remaining Clean Sisterhood went underground, giving their Mesoamerican idols the names of Christian saints and performing their rituals in secret. The Clean Sisterhood's patron goddess, *Tonantzin*, the mother of Precious Flower, became the Virgin Mother Guadalupe and Precious Flower became Mary Magdalene. Though the idols were now Christian, in the shadows the words the Clean Sisters whispered were still in the archaic tongue Grandfather Fire and their ancestral ghosts could understand.

Hidden in the Mountains of the Clouds and far from the watchful eyes of the Church, the Clean Sisters listened to the pulse of the land and kept the original Ghost Dance alive by performing the old calendar's ceremonies at specific times of the year. These ceremonies culminated every 52 years on June 18th, and the eventual manifestation of their Seven Generations Prophecy would rely on the completion of this ongoing cycle.

During the Inquisition many Clean Sisters were burned at the stake, along with almost all of the codices that held the histories of pre-Columbian knowledge. Paranoid and fearful of what they were sure was the devil's domain, the Inquisitors tried to completely erase the Mesoamerican cosmology from history with bonfires and book burnings. Every codex they found was to be burned, and the bearded and double-crowned Grandfather

Fire, the oldest of the gods, was mixed together with the satyr and transformed into the image of the European devil.

Through the illusionary smoke of his obsidian Black Mirror, *Tezcatlipoca*, Lord of Witches, remained hidden behind the scenes like a puppet master pulling strings, manipulating events to cover his tracks. *Tezcatlipoca* wanted the Catholic priests to erase his stories from their history so he could continue undisturbed with his plan to eliminate the barbarity of humanity from the Fifth World.

"My greatest illusion is convincing the conquerors that I am a myth," he told his most trusted priests.

CHAPTER 7
HE WALKED THE AMERICAS

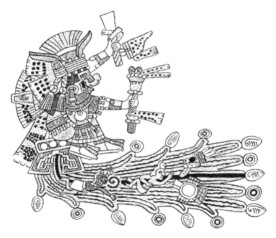

The Goddess of the Waters (Chalcihuitlicue)

A s the colonial era began, the ghostly Toltec Ghost Dancer finally reached the first petal of the Black Flower in the underworld. It was here that *Chalcihuitlicue*, the Goddess of the Waters with the Jade Skirt, resided. The Lady of the Waters baptized the Ghost Dancer, and when the Toltec rose from the waters he became aware that his descendants had been conquered. Fear of oblivion haunted him, but nevertheless the tattered and worn skeletal ghost was determined to continue the ritual of the Americas until its future completion, when the Rope of the Dead would be rewoven.

CABEZA DE VACA

In the year 1528, a tempest stirred the shifting tides, causing Captain Álvar Núñez Cabeza de Vaca to shipwreck on what is today known as Galveston Island, Texas. Cabeza de Vaca washed ashore just north of the same Veracruz beach where *Quetzalcoatl* had been predicted to return centuries earlier. Seven years after Cortés' conquest of the Aztec, Cabeza de Vaca would become the first foreigner since the original Stranger to perform the Ghost Dance in the Americas.

Though most of his crew had died during the shipwreck or were killed by local tribesmen, Cabeza de Vaca and his slave, Esteban, survived and soon ended up as captives in a native Avavares village. During a tribal gathering that took place a short time after Cabeza De Vaca's arrival, a beloved Avavares elder appeared to fall dead right in front of the Spaniard. The women began to wail, pulling at their hair. But something possessed Cabeza De Vaca and he knelt over the elder, giving him his last rites and making the sign of the cross.

"In the name of the Father, Son and Holy Ghost," he repeated over and over again, and then, as if by a miracle, the elder opened his eyes. The Avavares were now certain that Cabeza de Vaca could raise the dead, and in a matter of moments he went from captive to holy man. The Avavares honored Cabeza de Vaca by awarding him an entourage to accompany him on his pilgrimage. Over the next three years, Cabeza de Vaca and his escort headed east towards what is now Florida in search of gold but found none.

Instead, Cabeza de Vaca encountered a country completely free of the plagues of disease that had ravaged Europe and were now crippling Mexico. By the time he and his followers reached Florida, Cabeza de Vaca also realized that the natives had a far greater knowledge of medicinal plants than the Europeans. This led him to wonder if there was a hidden treasure of health in America, one far more valuable than precious metals and one that could help plague-ridden Europe.

But after failing to find any gold riches in Florida, Cabeza de Vaca decided to return to Texas and rejoin the conquest in Mexico. The journey southwest took him eight years, and during this time, Cabeza de Vaca's hair and beard grew long while his clothes became nothing more than rags hanging on his frail frame. Cabeza de Vaca's lost expedition zigzagged north and south across what would later become the southern United States. Along the way, he began to use the cures he had learned from one tribe on afflicted individuals in other tribes. In this manner, Cabeza de Vaca, an outsider, was able to weave intertribal botanical knowledge among feuding peoples.

Heading southwest towards Mexico, Cabeza de Vaca came upon the legendary Cities of Gold, or Cíbola, glittering in the New Mexico sunlight. Cíbola was actually the adobe fortress of the Pueblo tribes, and mica, not gold, proved to be the reflective particles in the mud walls.

But inside the Cíbola, Cabeza de Vaca found death rather than gold, as he had arrived in the middle of the first epidemic the Zuni had ever faced. The Mother of All Plagues was on the move and her introduced diseases had spread north with the traveling Tlaxcalan merchants. The Zuni believed that only the gods or witches could cause sickness and cure disease, so Cabeza De Vaca's timely arrival raised the question of whether he was a mortal, a witch or a god.

Confused by this stranger, the Zuni sought counsel from their cousins, the Hopi, who had been waiting for the arrival of the mythological, white prodigal son *Pahana*, since before the plagues arrived with the Tlaxcalan. Leery at first, the Hopi began to believe that the arrival of Cabeza de Vaca was prophetic.

So the Hopi climbed down inside the smoky shadows of the old *kiva* at Oraibi, where the *Kachinas* waited, huddled together with their strange faces from a different world peeking out. Cabeza de Vaca sat against the wall on the opposite side, watching the *Kachinas* closely. As the elders chanted, the Hopi priests and their visitor consumed basketfuls of fresh peyote cactus buttons. While they ate this harsh sacrament, an old Hopi storyteller began to intone the legend of *Pahana*.

"Long ago, there were two brothers, a red brother named Hopi and a white brother like this man, Cabeza de Vaca, named *Pahana*. The red brother taught the Hopi how to live within the weave of nature and the *Kachinas* favored him. *Pahana*, the white brother, was also a good man, but he had left his children behind to go on a quest to find the carved jaguar bones, called the *tiponi*, or the Magic Child. These bones would give authority over the land back to the Hopi, and authority over the land is the greatest gift the gods can bestow upon humans."

The elder storyteller continued, "Without their father's supervision, the white brother's children became arrogant and destructive, showing no respect for Mother Nature or her children. But the children of the Hopi believed that *Pahana* would one day return with the missing Olmec shard of jaguar bones, which would give them back the rightful authority to protect the land from *Pahana's* misbehaving children.

Over a flame, a Hopi priest asked for Grandfather Fire's blessing.

"Grandfather Fire, we ask you to call upon *Awanyu*, the Plumed Serpent spirit of *Pahana*, to show us if this is our lost brother or one of his sons."

In woven cotton kilts, with their long hair hanging down, the Hopi priests sprinkled corn pollen over a huge urn, and as Cabeza de Vaca watched, a Plumed Serpent puppet rose up from the urn and began to sway from side to side. The spirit that made the puppet rise asked Cabeza de Vaca if he had brought the *tiponi*, but not only did Cabeza de Vaca not understand Hopi, he also didn't have the *tiponi*.

Realizing this, the tribe now knew for certain that Cabeza de Vaca was not the prophet *Pahana*. Fearing that Cabeza de Vaca had brought the sickness that had ravaged the Hopi's cousins, the Zuni, Cabeza de Vaca was driven from Hopi territory. But it was already too late, as Coronado's troops were on their way, bringing the plague along with them.

Cabeza de Vaca's long spiritual journey through North America ended when he could not fulfill the Hopi prophecy. After traveling on foot for an unbelievable twenty-three thousand miles, a worn and disillusioned Cabeza de Vaca now turned away from the *Kachina's* home in the San Francisco Peaks, and instead walked south, in the direction of the conquest in Mexico.

THE PEYOTE EATERS

Through the present-day Mexican state of Sinaloa, Cabeza de Vaca continued on southward towards Nayarit. In the Sierra Nayarit, a particularly elusive tribe called the Vishalika intercepted him. The Vishalika later became better known by the name their enemies called them, the peyote eaters, or the Huichol.

Unlike the Hopi, the high priest of the Huichol believed that Cabeza de Vaca fulfilled their own Stranger prophecy, which was based on the original Stranger who had transformed into the Plumed Serpent.

Through a translator, the high priest told Cabeza de Vaca, "We have been waiting for you, you who have traveled the great Hoop of Life. You now bring to us what you have learned, so we, our Mother's Keepers, can protect the Tree of Life."

In recognition of his new role as the Huichol's Stranger, Cabeza de Vaca was initiated into the Huichol's own version of the Ghost Dance, one older even than the Aztec Lady of the Dead ceremony. After four days of purifications, the Clean Sisters of the Huichol prepared the Stranger for the ritual.

Cabeza de Vaca was dressed as an initiate and his face was painted so he would not appear naked before the ancestral ghosts. Inside a tribal circle created by the women, Cabeza de Vaca and other initiates sat before a *mara-akame*, as the tribal medicine man was called. The *mara-akame* chanted to commune with the oldest of the gods: Grandfather Fire who the Huichol's called *Tatewari*. Then the medicine man asked Grandfather Fire to infuse each initiate with the identity of an important departed ancestor.

The ancestral Spirit of the Americas now possessed Cabeza de Vaca, and as he took on the personality of this ghost, he was given a title: *peyotero*. Led by the *mara-akame* and guided by the ancestral ghost, Cabeza de Vaca left the Huichol's mountainous home on foot to follow the Rope of the Dead to *Wirikuta*, or the Land of the Precious Flower. The four hundred and twenty mile cyclical path followed the footsteps of *Quetzalcoatl* and traced the Huichol's spiritual Hoop of Life. Although they had no calendar, the Huichol *peyoteros* traveled the Rope of the Dead, following Venus to perform the necessary rituals at the right times and locations along their Hoop of Life.

After journeying for another two hundred miles, Cabeza de Vaca and the initiates finally arrived at a chaparral outside the area of Mexico now called San Luis Potosí. It was here, in *Wirikuta*, Land of the Precious Flower, that the Huichol sacramental peyote grew. When the travelers arrived at this place, the *mara-akame* made tobacco offerings to the Great Owl Hunters, another name for the Lord and Lady of the Dead.

After the offering, the *peyoteros* ate the first peyote cactus they found and bared their souls to the *mara-akame* until dusk. In this way, each *peyotero* would spiritually die to release himself from his position in life. Once released from his earthly bonds by the peyote, Cabeza de Vaca felt as if he was floating like a great bird towards Venus, the Evening Star. Here he found a dog that led him past the one-eyed, hunchbacked Grandmother, the Gatekeeper of the Milky Way.

When the clouds opened, the descending sun was still above the *peyoteros* and the spirit of Cabeza de Vaca followed this setting sun down into the underworld. Startled by his transformed state from nobleman to ascetic, Cabeza de Vaca fell through the torments of the Vision Serpent's throat. The sun's rays impregnated him with jaguar semen in the form of quartz crystals, ripping the flesh from his body like knives. Stripped bare of his human form, Cabeza de Vaca was now a fierce were-jaguar, just like the ancestral members of the Olmec jaguar cult.

When the sun rose the next morning, Cabeza de Vaca, still possessed by his jaguar totem, had the ability to track the hoof prints of the sacred deer, *Kauyumari*, which was the totem spirit of the peyote cactus. The Huichol's ancestors recognized that all deer were sacred because they were one of the few animals that lived without patterns or routines.

When the sacred deer led the *peyoteros* to the first abundance of the cactus, the *mara-akame* ceremonially shot a large peyote cactus with a tiny bow and arrow, signaling that peyote could then be collected for the ritual. After weeks of fasting and hard travel,

Cabeza de Vaca and the Huichol *peyoteros* collected hundreds of peyote buttons from the tops of the cactus and began the return journey to their own seven sacred caves: the caves of Terra Cotta.

Upon arriving, the wife or Clean Sister of each *peyotero* was waiting to greet and adorn them with eagle, parrot or hawk feathers. The *peyoteros* then put on their finest clothing, which had been woven by the women with images inspired by the peyote visions of their husbands.

At dusk, dressed in their sacred garments, Cabeza de Vaca and the *peyoteros* began a slow, shuffling dance around the *mara-akame* and his drummers. In the sacred land of Terra Cotta, the beat of that drum echoed and came out on the other side of the Cave of the Wind, where *Tezcatlipoca* watched the events unfold.

The women sat in a larger circle around the men, holding ghosts' eyes made of cotton yarn wrapped around two crossed sticks to defend the *peyoteros* against spiritual intrusions and opportunistic witches. The ritual continued through the night and into the next morning.

After two days of eating peyote in greater and greater quantities, Cabeza de Vaca noticed that the taste of the terribly bitter peyote had now transformed into the delicate flavor of a cactus pear.

As Cabeza de Vaca and the rest of the *peyoteros* continued to dance and eat peyote, the Kauyumari, the spirit of peyote, addressed Cabeza de Vaca. Hearing the plant speak, Cabeza de Vaca finally understood that the source of plant knowledge came from plants that had learned to communicate with humans. As Cabeza de Vaca listened to the talking plant, the medicine man continued to chant.

"I am a man of corn and only a man of corn can become a jaguar that hunts *Kauyumari*, the sacred deer. Now that I have the eyes of a jaguar I can see a day when the entire world will be beautiful again as it is in *Wirikuta*, Land of the Precious Flower and then, all our ancestors will return."

The Ghost Dance ritual of the Huichol had brought Cabeza de Vaca's entire journey into perspective, as Cabeza de Vaca had spoken with a talking plant and had become a Ghost Dancer of the Americas. With his spiritual journey now complete, Cabeza de Vaca and his slave Esteban wandered southward. By the time they reached the newly founded Mexico City, Cortés had become governor.

Brought before Cortés and his entourage, a straggly Cabeza de Vaca pleaded his case.

"*Señores*, there is a treasure even greater than gold in this land, for these people still remember what we Europeans have forgotten, how to live as part of nature in the Garden of Eden. Take your gold, but leave its people in peace."

Cortés and the viceroy, Antonio de Mendoza, looked at Cabeza de Vaca as a madman and had no understanding of what he was trying to communicate. Instead, all they could see was a traitor who had gone native. Although Cortés remained completely unaware of *Quetzalcoatl* and *Tezcatlipoca's* hidden agendas, in Cabeza de Vaca he recognized a threat to his conquest of the New World.

Cortés rid himself of the problem of Cabeza de Vaca by handing the tired traveler orders to return to Spain and report his expedition's findings. When Cabeza de Vaca arrived home, he found that the Spanish Crown was not impressed with his report because they were not interested in natural history, anthropology or the devil's work with talking plants; they only wanted gold.

Álvar Núñez Cabeza de Vaca never returned to the American continent he had grown to love. Instead, he lived out his life in obscurity as a schoolteacher. Cabeza de Vaca was unable to rise up fully and be transformed into a Plumed Serpent.

Nonetheless, he was among the first Europeans who truly understood what it was to be American.

CHAPTER 8
FOUNDING FATHERS AND ANGRY WITCHES

The Ghost Dancer

T he Ghost Dance lay dormant in the earth of the Americas for another century and a half. But while the great Plumed Serpent slept, the ghost of the Toltec Ghost Dancer continued to follow the footprints of his patron god through the underworld and into the next petal of the Black Flower: the desert realm of *Tlaltecuhtlia.*

This was the Land of Unfulfilled Dreams, where lost souls wandered for eternity. The Toltec Ghost Dancer might easily have become lost forever because the ground in this area of the underworld was dry and hard, and the Plumed Serpent's trail had become increasingly less visible. But, using his instincts, the Toltec Ghost Dancer eventually found his footing and was led beyond the desert to a forgotten city.

Popay

By 1680, the Spanish crown was firmly established in Santa Fe, New Mexico, and the King of Spain had put the Franciscan monks in charge of evangelizing the Pueblo tribes. The Franciscans used the Spanish troops to subjugate the Pueblo people and turn them into a slave labor force. To scare any resistant Pueblo tribal member, the Spaniards hunted down and cut off the left foot of all those who fought back.

Listening to the wisdom of their ancestors, the medicine men of the San Juan Pueblo tribe launched a small revolt. To put down the revolt, the governor, Juan Francisco Trevino, had his troops sack the sacred *kivas*, destroying any ritual objects they could find. Then Trevino arrested all the Pueblo holy men, including a rebel named Popay, and charged them with witchcraft.

From the time the Spanish had arrived with Coronado, Popay, a medicine man from the San Juan Pueblo, fiercely resisted their intrusion. Popay was a stout and somber man with dark, brooding eyes framed by facial features that resembled the ancient Olmec. For his rebellious acts, Governor Trevino had Popay publically whipped and imprisoned in a dungeon, where Popay planned an escape. From the jail, the wily Popay sent out false information through evangelized Indian spies. He counted on this information falling into the hands of the governor and predicted that Trevino would respond with a show of force.

Popay's instincts soon proved correct. As Governor Trevino ordered most of the Spanish garrison out on maneuvers in response to the false intelligence he had received, few guards were left behind at the stockade, and the imprisoned medicine men easily overpowered them and broke out of prison.

After the escape of this medicine-man brigade, Popay and his followers hid in the mountains below the Taos Pueblo. There Popay fasted and allowed the elements of nature to break him down until he was possessed by an ancestral ghost. The ghost showed Popay the ritual he needed to perform to unite his people. This ritual was a version of the Ghost Dance based on the *Awanyu* Plumed Serpent, the Pueblo people's symbol of the phallic power of the universe. The difference between the more ancient Ghost Dance of Mexico and the Hopi Ghost Dance was that once the ritual entered North America, the local tribes used means other than plant-based sacraments to access their sacred visions.

Many who attended Popay's Ghost Dance later said, "We have seen the totem of our people dancing with Popay."

Popay understood that the Ghost Dance was a gift from the ancestors to help the Indian people continue past the hell the Europeans had brought down upon them.

"We must survive because we follow the gods' path. We are clean and respect all living things. The Spanish are dirty, riddled with disease; they are an abomination of nature. They have no respect for the Mother and only worship dead things. The ancestral ghosts have instructed me on how to drive the Spanish out of our land, " Popay told the people.

Obeying the ancestors' instructions, Popay became a leader in the Pueblo resistance against the Spanish. He sent runners to spread the fomenting seeds of revolt among the people and in this way he was able to unify the constantly bickering Pueblo tribes for the first time. Then, with the Pueblo tribes united behind him, Popay began to orchestrate his next plan of attack. He prayed to the Lord of the Wind to blow away the clouds and bring a drought down upon the land. Unused to living in such barren surroundings, the Spaniards soon wilted, while the Pueblo, who knew how to endure drought conditions, survived. Then the united Pueblo tribes drove the sun-dried Spaniards out and reclaimed authority over the land. That same year, the rains returned.

The Pueblo Revolt of 1680 was the first successful overthrow of European dominance in North America by a native people. This was also the first time the Ghost Dance was linked to an armed resistance. Over the next twelve years, Popay systematically rid his land of the Spanish while reinstating traditional beliefs. But although Popay's revolt allowed him to reclaim his land for his people, he still could not prevent the Mother of All Plagues from spreading the epidemics brought by the *conquistadores*.

Somewhere around 1693, Popay, like his tutelary spirit the Plumed Serpent, wandered off into the mountains below the Taos Pueblo and mysteriously disappeared. With Popay gone, the Spanish returned to their stronghold in Santa Fe and instated a new governor, Diego de Vargas, who approached the conquest of the Pueblo people in a relatively more humane manner than his predecessors. "Convert the heathens with metal and commerce rather than torture and physical bloodshed," de Vargas ordered his soldiers.

So with de Vargas' support, the Spanish once again began trading popular metal goods such as knives, farming tools, axes and metal pots with the Pueblo of the Southwest. Unfortunately for the pueblo, the consequence of this open-minded free trade was a greater level of exposure to the infectious diseases brought to the New World by the Europeans. After the Pueblo Revolt ended, the Ghost Dance once again faded from history and its Plumed Serpent remained dormant in the soil of the Americas for another calendar Short Cycle of fifty-two years.

CHAPTER 9
THE ANCESTOR DANCE

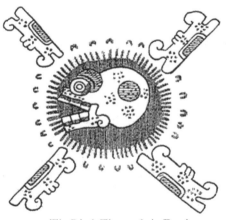

The Black Flower of the Dead

F rom out of the dust of a million bones, the footprints of the Plumed Serpent, *Quetzalcoatl*, now appeared. The lost Toltec Ghost Dancer, elated at finding direction in the Black Flower below, followed his god's footsteps into the underworld caverns of the god *Centeotl*. It was here that the red ant had found the first kernel of corn and it was also where *Tezcatlipoca* had chosen to hide the *tiponi*, the carved jaguar bones that could return authority over the land to the local tribes.

Deep in the bowels of the underworld, neither the ghostly Toltec Ghost Dancer nor his faithful dog could find the *tiponi* by sight, scent or sound. For the Ghost Dancer to succeed, he now had to use the senses he had developed in the forgotten desert: feeling and seeing with only his mind's eye. Stumbling in the dank and stagnant cavern passages, the Toltec Ghost Dancer felt his patron god whisper in the form of a gentle breeze that tickled the back of his neck. Bending down, he touched the ground and felt the tip of a bone hidden in the dust.

But just as he was about to pick up the engraved bone, the sticky bullwhip tongue of the giant toad lashed out, blocking his way to the sacred treasure. Racing around the toad's slippery tongue, the Toltec's dog snatched the bone and ran, hiding in the shadows of the dark petal of the Black Flower, as the Toltecs' patron god *Quetzalcoatl* had done long ago.

Clutching the sacred jaguar bone tightly, the Toltec and his hound raced down the path, following in *Quetzalcoatl's* footsteps. As the Toltec Ghost Dancer hurried, he stumbled and fell, accidently breaking the sacred bone of the *tiponi* into seven pieces in the same way *Quetzalcoatl* had once long ago broken the bones of the Grateful Dead. Collecting the pieces, the Toltec then hid them among the ancestral ghosts of seven tribes. This was done so that future Ghost Dancers would be able to find the seven different rituals that make up the Ghost Dance by following the Rope of the Dead to the seven tribes who had been keeping the dance alive. When the ritual was complete, it would fulfill the prophecy of Seven Generations by healing the Tree of Life. As the Toltec ghost hid the bones, a new Ghost Dancer appeared among the Algonquin people in the world of the living.

THE ENLIGHTENED ONE

In 1749, a Delaware medicine man, whose name Neolin meant "enlightened one" in the Algonquin dialect, observed the arrival of the European settlers. Neolin's proximity to the French and Dutch trappers along the Ohio River allowed him to learn several languages and also exposed the curious tribesman to stories from the Bible.

Amazed by the similarities between the Delaware people's prophets and the great healer Jesus, Neolin was also intrigued to learn that Moses could read messages from God written in stone just like the Delaware holy men could do. Although Neolin took to the newcomers' religious stories, he began to question the filth and squalor of their mission outposts as he watched the trappers cut down and pollute the forest around them.

Neolin began to realize that the trading posts he had come to enjoy so much were where the Delaware contracted the diseases that were taking a severe toll on his people. The cholera epidemic that had originated at the missions was spread by a lack of basic sanitation and was worsened by a huge influx of immigrants. Indians were put in contact with the European diseases when they came to the trading posts to buy metal tools, and then returned to their villages carrying the invisible and deadly germs. The missionaries explained the epidemics as their One True God punishing the Indians for their heathen ways.

A brooding Neolin was tormented, confronted with a problem that only the ancestral ghosts could answer. On a stormy night in 1754, Neolin stood alone on a sacred mound seeking a vision. For the second time in the history of the Ghost Dance, there was no seed of the Fruit of Knowledge or other visionary sacrament to use to commune with the ancestors through the Rope of the Dead.

Instead, Neolin fasted and prayed. "Grandfather, can you hear me? I humbly come to you for the tribe, not for myself. How do we stop these plagues that the white witches have cast upon us?"

Fasting and singing allowed Neolin's mind to reach out past the boundaries of reality and into the spirit world. He then had a vision of the supreme spirit of the Delaware people, called *Keesh-she-la-mil-lang*, or the Master of Life. Neolin believed that it was this Master of Life himself rather than the ancestral ghosts who had spoken to him and taught him the Ghost Dance. The Master of Life told Neolin that the Europeans he had befriended would ultimately destroy the Delaware people.

Touched by the spirit of the Master of Life, Neolin held a dance to bring his vision to the tribe. These ritual dances of the Delaware went all the way back to the Aztec roots shared by many of the tribes of the eastern coast of North America. The dance steps had arrived with the corn brought by the Clean Sisterhood centuries before. But whether Neolin had actually learned the concept of ghost dancing from the Master of Life or from oral tradition, his version of the Ghost Dance would soon become a hybrid of what he had been taught by his own tradition and what he had learned from Christianity.

It was obvious, dressed as they were in their finest for the dance, that the Delaware people had been influenced by the Dutch traders. The young and fashion-conscious Delaware had replaced traditional, naturally dyed porcupine quills and shells with brightly colored imported beads, cloth and pieces of tin. Without realizing it, the Delaware people were already being influenced by a modern consumer mentality, hoping to attract mates with the latest trends in brightly colored bobbles and beads.

Neolin himself wore only a single strand of imported beads around his neck. When he entered the circle to dance, the drums played and he moved slowly around the fire. His shadow was like a ghost in the flickering flames, possessed as he was by his vision of the Master of Life.

Long hours into the night, the Delaware danced until the vision came. In the early morning, the drums abruptly stopped and Neolin spoke. "*Keesh-she-la-mil-lang*, the Master of Life, told me that everything the settlers have brought, including their adornments and beads, are polluted and will ultimately cause us great harm. The Master of Life says that the white man is not a great conqueror. He is just the dirty dog that has carried the Plague Mother's fleas of conquest from across the sea. The Master of Life has instructed us to throw all of the white man's polluted objects into Grandfather's fire and return to our traditional ways."

Then Neolin ripped his bead necklace from his neck and threw it into the fire. The Delaware youth, shocked by his actions, did not follow his example.

Confused, a young brave questioned Neolin. "I do not understand why the Master of Life would give us things he did not want us to use. It takes many days to cut down a large tree with a stone axe, but with a metal one it only takes half a day. This gives our people more time to do what we like the most: hunting, dancing and spending time with our families. Why is this bad?"

Like the other Eastern tribes, the Delaware people had already grown accustomed to the metal axes, pots, knives and other tools of the white man and were not willing to give them up, prophecy or no prophecy.

But as the plague brought by the Europeans ravaged the Delaware people, Neolin's words struck a chord, and his following began to grow. In 1763, the colonists, growing more aware of Neolin's impact, dubbed his movement the Nativist Revival. The main ceremony of the movement, Neolin's interpretation of the Ghost Dance, came to be called the Ancestor Dance.

Ironically, by focusing on the One God, *Keesh-she-la-mil-lang*, Neolin's Nativist Revival Movement had taken on the undertones of the fundamentalist missionaries he had become obsessed with driving out. It appeared the more Neolin changed the tradition, the more he seemed to lose his way. As Neolin's popularity waned, he began selling as religious artifacts pieces of bark inscribed with illiterate nonsense. Neolin was no longer a noble savage. Instead, he had become an opportunistic zealot.

Seeking allies, Neolin brought his Ancestor Dance to Chief Pontiac and his people, the Ottawa, who at that time were the most powerful tribe in the Ohio Territory. At the first Ottawan Ancestor Dance, Neolin declared, "You complain that the animals of the forest are few and scattered. You destroy them yourselves for their skins only and leave their bodies to rot or give the best pieces to the whites. You must kill no more animals than are necessary to feed and clothe yourselves."

With Chief Pontiac's support, the second organized militant resistance of the tribes of North America (the first being the resistance led by Popay) began with a form of the Ghost Dance. Pontiac was a brilliant strategist and quickly won the war using a divide-and-conquer strategy, playing the German, Dutch and French invaders against each other while employing the guns and ammunition the Indians received from the British.

By February of 1765, the French and Indian War had ended and the vast majority of foreign troops were expelled from the tribal lands of the Ottawa and the Delaware. Only Neolin's allies, the British, were allowed to remain, and their hardnosed leader, General Amherst, led his victorious army back to Fort Pitts.

Soon after, Amherst received letters from his commanding officers instructing him to give blankets to the Ottawa and Delaware peoples as a sign of friendship between comrades-in-arms. But the blankets he eventually sent had been collected from smallpox hospital wards.

As Amherst's superiors had hoped, a smallpox epidemic hit the Ottawa and Delaware peoples with a deadly fury. Drunken young braves, demoralized by the impact of the disease, turned their flintlock rifles on each other, fighting over a rapidly vanishing female population. As the Delaware and Ottawa populations imploded, their grandmothers traveled from one band to the next in a desperate attempt to stop the infighting.

The grandmothers were the only ones in the tribe who were capable of ending feuds; a man of authority would be killed were he sent to talk peace and a young woman would be abducted. The female elders were considered to be the natural choice to conduct peace talks because they not only had life experience and more intertribal relations than anyone else, they also were unlikely to be used as a threat or a trophy.

Considered to be tools of peace, the neutrality of these women of wisdom allowed them to travel freely in times of war. Female peacemakers were a dynamic part of the early Native American cultures, but despite their powerful presence, even the grandmothers were not able to mediate a resolution in this time of drastic change.

Almost twenty years after Neolin first performed the Ancestor Dance, he called together all the remaining bands of Delaware and Ottawa people for a large gathering. As Neolin spoke to his sick and dying people, he revealed his latest vision, a vision that once again shook the tribes to their very core. "The

Master of Life has changed his mind and now orders the Delaware and the Ottawa to lay down their flintlocks." Neolin then took his own rifle and threw it into the Grandfather's fire.

Pontiac was outraged and felt deeply betrayed by Neolin, questioning his motives. "It is you, not the Master of Life who has changed his mind. The Spirit knows, as I do, that there is little hope for any of the tribes if we give up our rifles."

Neolin's answer to Pontiac was somber and humble. "My brother, I understand how you feel, but the Master of Life has shown me there is nothing we can do that will change the course of our destiny. Life has both times of joy and times of pain, and this is a time when our people must suffer. We will be ground down on the stone of life, but it will give us the edge to save our future generations. Only when the Seven Generations Prophecy is fulfilled will the ancestral ghost return to teach humans how to live instead of die."

After this confrontation, Neolin never performed the Ancestor Dance again. Without Neolin's support, Chief Pontiac was unable to keep the intruders out, and so the European settlers flooded back into the eastern Ohio Territory. This disagreement between Neolin and Pontiac ended not only the Nativist Revival Movement, but also the indigenous uprising that later became known as Pontiac's Rebellion. Without the help of the Ancestor Dance, the defeat of Chief Pontiac raised deep questions among the tribes of the Appalachian, Delaware and the eastern Ohio Territory.

CHAPTER 10
THE PROPHET DANCE

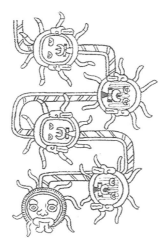

The Rope of the Dead

The ghost of the Toltec Ghost Dancer entered a new petal of awareness. In this petal there was no struggle and the lessons were pleasant. This was a place where a Ghost Dancer would be honored for giving his life to the Rope of the Dead. Many trinkets and bobbles were given, and the more the Toltec received, the more he wanted. Here the Ghost Dancer welcomed praise, even though praise made him weaker. Realizing he was losing his edge, he returned to the path the Rope of the Dead had laid out for him.

OPEN DOOR

Before becoming a Ghost Dancer, the one-eyed, younger brother of the famous Shawnee Chief Tecumseh was called the Noise Maker because he was a loud and obnoxious drunk. When his self-proclaimed mentor, the great Shawnee medicine man Penagashea died, the Noise Maker was deeply saddened and sought spiritual guidance. Traveling to Ottawan territory in search of answers, he attended Neolin's last Ancestor Dance. At this Ancestor Dance, Neolin's predictions of hopelessness made the Noise Maker even more depressed.

Arriving back at his village, the Noise Maker got so drunk he blacked out and fell into an open fire. After pulling him from the fire, his brother Tecumseh thought him dead and began to prepare him for burial. But suddenly the Noise Maker opened his one good eye and returned to life. In a trance state, the still-smoldering Noise Maker stood up and shuffled about, doing his own version of the Ancestor Dance he had learned at Neolin's last Nativist Revival meeting. When the Noise Maker returned from his trance he shared his vision with his tribe.

"I have spoken with the One God above all others. *Keesh-she-la-mil-lang*, the Master of Life, has told me that the Shawnee must wage war on the settlers and drive them out before it is too late."

Few listened to his drunken ravings at first, and others were offended by his pompous arrogance, but after this prophetic vision the Noise Maker went through a complete metamorphosis. He stopped drinking and changed his name to Tenskwatawa, or Open Door. Tenskwatawa began to hold traditional revivals where he danced his own, more aggressive version of Neolin's

Ancestor Dance and chanted, "Master of Life, give us the weapons we need to drive out the foreigners."

Open Door's brother, Chief Tecumseh, also wanted guns to protect his tribe from the white invader, knowing that the Shawnee would not survive a cavalry attack without them. The Shawnee were originally one of the Central-Eastern tribes pushed west of the Appalachian Mountains and Ohio River by the infamous and sadistic Andrew Jackson.

In 1804, Andrew Jackson helped negotiate the Louisiana Purchase, opening the door for the first white settlers to move west of the Ohio River. In these wide-open spaces, providence seemed to look favorably upon the indigenous refugees; it was here that they discovered herds of feral horses called mustangs left behind by the Spanish. Rounding up and domesticating the mustangs not only gave the Shawnee a new strategic edge, but the horses also provided a powerful opportunity to barter with the British. The British were eager to trade rifles for horses that they needed to build up their own cavalry, in an attempt to keep both the French and American colonists out of the territory.

Open Door's prayers were answered and the guns arrived, but another problem remained. Chief Tecumseh was unable to unify the feuding Shawnee tribes without a spiritual leader. Though Tecumseh's brother, Open Door, claimed to be a holy man, he had no followers. But when white colonists flooded into the region, the frightened Shawnee went in search of answers and found Open Door waiting. When the Shawnee came to dance with Open Door, Tecumseh was so impressed with his brother's transformation that he made him his holy man, renaming him the Prophet. Soon after the Prophet received his new name, his version of Neolin's Ancestor Dance became known as the Prophet Dance.

What the Prophet lacked in personality and beauty, he compensated for by wearing fancy European clothes. The young people loved his trendy attire and flocked to him. Having their ear gave the Prophet the stage he had always wanted and he now spoke with authority and conviction.

"The Master of Life has shown me that the wild game will vanish just before the white man's witches send the epidemics of disease. Our fight is not *Seven Generations* from now, it is *right* now. If we do not stop the intruders today, there will be no future for the Shawnee."

With great insight, Tecumseh took advantage of his brother's popularity and turned the masses of discontented young braves who came to his brother's Prophet Dance into a guerilla army. With a highly evolved strategy instigated by the Prophet Dance and aided by horses, Tecumseh began to drive the invading settlers out. Backed by their allies, the Shawnee soon began to win almost every battle they fought against the white colonists, becoming more successful at pushing out the invader than even Pontiac had been.

Excited by their success and his own rising fame, the Prophet took Neolin's version of the Ghost Dance one step further. His rhetoric became an explosive mixture of Seven Generation fervor and the fire-and-brimstone scripture he had learned from the missionaries.

"I need no ancestors to speak for me. The Master of Life has chosen me over all others to speak to him directly. Soon, the Master of Life will make the earth shake and this will topple all the buildings of the white man. Then, it will rain for many moons and a great flood will come to wash all their filth away, including their domesticated animals and they themselves will be swept away. When the earth is cleansed, the native people will come down from the trees and live as they did before. Until that day we must show the Master of Life that we are on his side by helping him to drive the invader out."

Though Tecumseh was uneasy with his brother's lack of humility in speaking of the ancestors, he overlooked it as their following grew.

General William Henry Harrison, the governor of the Indiana Territory, feared Tecumseh, but he was certain that the Prophet was a fraud. Harrison became determined to usurp Tecumseh's spell over the Indian people before they could drive all the whites out of the Ohio and Indiana Territories.

In an effort to both embarrass and discredit the Prophet, Harrison publicly dared him to prove his power by carrying out a miracle. The Prophet accepted the challenge and his moment in the sun came in 1806, when, for an unknown reason, the Prophet made the Prophet Dance a daytime ceremony. With Harrison and other spectators watching, the day turned to night as the moon moved to block out the sun in a full solar eclipse. The Prophet's "miracle" caused Harrison's plan to backfire and this amazing event became a legend.

Whether or not the Prophet actually foresaw the eclipse or was tipped off beforehand ultimately didn't matter. His success provided Tecumseh with an opportunity to finally unite the remaining tribes of the vast Ohio Territory. Hundreds now flocked to the Prophet Dance, preparing to drive the last handful of settlers out of the Ohio Territory.

The Prophet and Tecumseh's following had now become so large that the village at Greenville could no longer support the huge numbers of people who gathered to drive the white man out. So in 1808, Tecumseh and the Prophet moved their people to the more fertile Prophetstown, near the Wabash and Tippecanoe Rivers in the Indiana Territory.

Fueled by revenge, Harrison waited until his spies told him that Tecumseh was away supporting the British in a battle against the French, and then made his move. Just as Harrison had predicted, without Tecumseh's help, the Prophet proved to be an extremely poor commander. General Harrison uprooted the Shawnee from their homes, salted their earth and destroyed all of their food supplies so they could not survive the winter. The Prophet ran and hid as the captured braves, women and children were publicly mutilated.

When Techumseh returned and witnessed the carnage, he was enraged at his brother's lack of judgment. It became clear to Tecumseh that the people were abandoned at Prophetstown because the Prophet had insulted the ancestral ghosts by claiming he could speak to the Master of Life directly and, therefore, did not need their aid.

Tecumseh believed his only hope was to gain back the support of the ancestral ghosts, so the warrior chief went on his own vision quest. He performed a traditional Shawnee Ghost Society ceremony to seek the advice of the ancestral ghosts. During Tecumseh's ceremony, the ancestral ghosts came to him and forgave his brother's insults, telling him that as long as the people respected them, the ancestors would help the Shawnee drive the invaders out.

Over the next two years, Tecumseh amassed over four thousand braves and with the arms supplied to the Shawnee by the British, every last white settler was driven out of the Ohio Territory. News of Tecumseh's victories quickly spread a powerful spark of hope throughout the Native American world. The Prophet was then sent back East to sow further seeds of rebellion among the already-conquered tribes.

As Tecumseh stopped the colonial expansion westward, the Eastern tribes followed him and began to drive the white settlers back to their eastern cities. But just when it seemed like a definitive victory was at hand, the British lost the War of 1812 and stopped supplying the Shawnee warriors with the guns and ammunition they had come to depend on. Neolin's prophecy from fifty-two years earlier now seemed to be coming to pass. As Neolin had warned Pontiac, "The rifles are as polluted as all the other things the white man brings, and sooner or later they will betray us."

Neolin was proven right. Though the white man's rifles had given the Shawnee victory, they ultimately brought defeat. In 1813, Tecumseh was mortally wounded at the Battle of the Thames by the troops of his old adversary, General Harrison, and the last hope of driving out the invader vanished.

CHAPTER 11
THE DREAMER

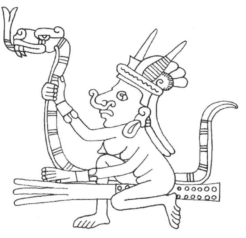

The Goddess of Witches (Tlazolteotl)

Lost, the Toltec Ghost Dancer walked in a circle, returning to the petal of the Black Flower of *Tlazolteotl*, the giant toad, where he had once survived the goddess' deadly tongue. *Tlazolteotl* ruled over her domain with a lust and passion so powerful, she caused mountains to collide and blood to flow like rivers. *Tlazolteotl* was also the goddess of menstruation, purification and blood magic.

Here, the Toltec Ghost Dancer would have to face any past sexual misconduct he had committed while he was alive. Because his sins were mild, he escaped being crushed by her Colliding Mountains and evaded her River of Blood. But even so, the goddess still questioned the purity of his intentions.

Flying on her sacred broom, the Eater of Filth circled the Ghost Dancer. She shrouded him in a mist of desire so thick that he was not able to see even his own skeletal hand in front of his face. The Toltec Ghost Dancer stumbled through the mist, consumed by the sensuality of his own imagination and completely unaware of his surroundings.

Hidden in that mist, the Left-Handed Hummingbird, the Aztec god of conquest, revenge and the sun, had transformed himself into the Lord of the Obsidian Knife, the god who consumes the life force around still-beating human hearts. Although the Left-Handed Hummingbird had been adapted into the Toltec religion, he had also enslaved the Toltec people's descendants and wished to do the same to the Toltecs' last Ghost Dancer.

With a slash of his obsidian knife, the Left-Handed Hummingbird cut the skeletal Toltec Ghost Dancer in half from head to toe, creating two independent sides of the same individual. The vengeful god hoped that the Ghost Dancer would come to hate the other side of himself so much that he would self-destruct. But instead, the Ghost Dancer turned to face his other half, and together they continued on the journey to mend the Rope of the Dead.

SMOHALLA

In 1863, the Civil War broke out and the United States was divided as brother learned to hate brother. Ironically, this gave the Indians of the western territories a momentary reprieve, as white men focused on killing each other. For nearly a full cycle of the ancient calendar, the Ghost Dance vanished from the landscape. But an indigenous revival would soon emerge from the calm at the center of the storm. This revival would arise from a Ghost Dance performed by a Wanapum medicine man named Smohalla.

Smohalla, known as the Dreamer, had wise eyes and a hunched back. Dreamers were believed to be able to see both into the future and the past using their dreams. For the Amerindians, dreams were a place where many of the problems of the waking world could be rectified in a buffer zone between the living and the dead.

But Smohalla's own dreams were shattered when his beloved daughter died tragically. At her funeral he keeled over, seeming to die of a broken heart. Just as his family was about to perform his funeral rites, Smohalla, like the Prophet before him, opened his eyes and returned to the world of the living. Smohalla had come back from the world of dreams with a vision and a new ritual for his tribe that he claimed would deliver them from the suffering brought on by the diseases of the invaders.

"In my dream, I traveled across the Milky Way to the Land of the Dead, but upon reaching this place, the ancestral ghosts would not let me in. They directed me to return to the living and to teach the people the song and dance that I had learned from them. The ancestors told me that violent resistance would not drive the polluters out, but if we danced their dance, in Seven Generations, the ancestral ghosts would bring the totem spirit out of hibernation to cleanse this land. What we must do is bring the feathered serpent through our dreams with this ritual."

In many ways, Smoholla's new ritual was a return to the old tradition of communing with the gods through the ancestors rather than communing solely with the Master of Life. Smoholla also brought back the Prophecy of Seven Generations, taking it as a literal interpretation of a specific length of time. Smoholla came to this decision after Tecumseh's downfall, seeing no hope in encouraging the tribes to prepare for an armed defense of their land and believing that fate rather than bullets would mark the destiny of the tribes.

According to Smolhalla's vision, the only way the tribes would survive was by returning the Indian people's ancestral totem, the Plumed Serpent, to the ritual dance. Like the Toltec, Smohalla believed that the totem of the people, rather than the ghosts of their ancestors, would ultimately heal the people and their ravaged land. Smoholla's ritual came to be known as the *Washani Nagai*, or Ghost Dance.

The Ghost Dance was the name that the Shaker missionaries called all of the Native American reclaiming rituals, but in the Wanapum dialect, these two words had a deeper meaning. The word *washani* meant both dance and ritual simultaneously. When the words *nagai* and *washani* were joined together to form the expression Ghost Dance, the words took on a unique significance because the Wanapum word for ghost, *nagai*, implied a specific kind of ghost. A *nagai* was an animal totem spirit of a person or a tribe of people, just as the Plumed Serpent was the totem spirit of the Mesoamerican people. Smohalla's ritual was intended to gain wisdom from the ancestors so that the people could become one with the totem Spirit of the Americas once again.

At the moment between the time when the animals of the day go to sleep and those of night awaken, seven *kookoolot* drums began to play. To the beat of the *kookoolot* drums, first the Wanapum men and then the women began to shuffle backward, counterclockwise, moving back in time, instead of forward, as they circled around Smohalla. The dancers carried swan and eagle feathers, which represented the serpent's flight of transformation from the earth to the heavens, and they sang the songs that Smohalla had brought back from his dreams. "Grandfather, please, do not forsake your children. Send the *nagai* to cleanse the land, send the *nagai* to cleanse this land," Smohalla sang.

Smohalla continued to dance as he sang, carrying the curious European symbol of his ritual, a triangular flag with a five-pointed star centered on a red circle with a white, yellow, and blue background. As the Wanapum followed their Dreamer, a brass bell was also rung in time to the drumbeat, symbolizing the beating of the heart. Finally, after hours of dancing, the dancers entered a trance. Then Smohalla, who was normally shy and stoic, became possessed by spirits in the night and shook in ecstatic rapture before entering a dream state.

This type of communion with the Christian's Holy Spirit was foreign to the participants. At first they watched in fear, worried that their Dreamer was possessed by demons. But then Smohalla awoke from his dream and spoke of his vision.

"I have seen a giant black buffalo with steam coming out of its nostrils that will consume all the other buffalo in its path. When they are gone, so will we be gone, but the *nagai* will bring us back in Seven Generations."

Smohalla's giant black buffalo turned out to be the locomotive, and as his predictions came true and the buffalo died, more and more Indians from all over the Columbia Plateau region, including the Paiute and Chief Joseph and his Nez Percé, flocked to Smohalla's Ghost Dance.

Although these tribes believed Smohalla was performing an ancient ritual, he had not learned about shaking from fellow dreamers or from the ancestral ghosts. Instead, he had learned it from the cult of fundamentalist missionaries called the Shakers.

When Smohalla was a young man, the Shakers had come to the Wanapum Reservation to evangelize the tribes of the West. The Shakers' plan was to push out the Catholic Jesuits who had controlled many of these tribes since the conquest first arrived in North America. Because Smohalla was born with a hunched back, he could not hunt with the rest of the boys, and so he spent a lot of time in the village conversing with these missionaries and watching their strange ceremonies.

Smohalla came to believe that the missionaries' ritual shaking was the ceremony that the ancestors had taught him in his dream and he incorporated shaking into the Wanapum belief system.

FISH LAKE JOE

The gossip of the "moccasin grapevine" had begun to spread regarding the many different Ghost Dance reclaiming ceremonies springing up on reservations all across the country. As the revival grew, a new form of Native American belief system began to take shape: a fusion of the remaining Indian beliefs with a strong Christian doctrine. This hybrid would soon become the religion most Native Americans would follow into the next century. But one tribe, the Paiute, resisted this Christian invasion and continued to cling to the old ways.

The Paiute were a nomadic tribe from the region of Nevada who had roamed as far north as Smohalla's Columbia Plateau and south into Mexico. They were perceived as notorious healers, witches and dream walkers by the other tribes. During the Civil War, the Paiute traveled around the country searching for reclaiming rituals which could then be used to communicate with the ancestors.

The first Paiute to come and ghost dance on the Wanapum Reservation in southern Washington was a striking man with long gray hair named Horthorne Wodzaiwob and nicknamed Fish Lake Joe. At first Joe was drawn in by the Dreamer's ceremony and believed the ghost of the ancestral totem would rise up from the earth right before his eyes. But Fish Lake Joe started to wonder if the reason these reclaiming rituals were not fulfilling the Prophecy of Seven Generations was because they were being performed incorrectly.

Fish Lake Joe believed that Smohalla knew the steps of the dance and that was why he could dream the future. However, he also thought that Smohalla's ceremonies were incomplete because the Wanapum Dreamer did not use any of the proper Ghost Dance sacraments in his ritual. The plants originally used in the ritual did not grow on Wanapum land, located in the northern Columbian Plateau, but Fish Lake Joe knew just where to find them.

Joe brought the concept of Smohalla's Shaker-style Ghost Dance home to the Walker River Paiute Reservation. But during the time that Joe had been gone, the Shaker cult had already arrived at the reservation. Because of the Paiute's reputation as witches, the Shakers, like all the missionaries out West, believed that the Paiute represented the largest threat to evangelization in North America. What the missionaries feared most was the secret source of the Paiute ancient knowledge: the missing sacrament, or the Talking Plants.

The Paiute people, unlike the other tribes, had constantly crossed back and forth over that invisible line of Pan-American mysticism along the border between the United States and Mexico. This line had created a cultural break between the tribes above and below the border. From Mexico to the tip of South America's Amazon rainforest, the use of visionary psychotropic plants like the Little Ones was the source of the Southern peoples' mysticism. But more or less north of the Mexico border in the United States and up into Canada, the tribes used techniques such as sweats, fasting and bleeding to achieve a visionary state rather than plants.

Although the Northern tribes had adopted the Mesoamerican ceremonies, they did not inherit their psychotropic sacraments because the various Talking Plants did not grow much in the northern part of the Americas. Instead, the Northern tribes employed methods that would give them the closest experience to the effect produced by a sacramental psychotropic plant.

Though Fish Lake Joe had figured out that the traditional sacrament was missing from the ritual, he had no way of knowing which plant to use. So Joe decided to choose a plant that he was familiar with called *Toloache* (also known as Datura or jimsonweed) which the Paiute witches often used.

Believing that he was on a mission from the gods, Joe traveled from the plateau and across the prairie to bring his new Ghost Dance ceremony to the Paiute in Nevada. Along the way he watched the destruction of the Great Plains escalate as the railroads crept westward toward Paiute territory. Joe could not help but remember Smohalla's prediction that the people's end would come with the train.

Jay Gould, one of the financial principals behind the Union Pacific Railroad, had purposely created a land rush, bringing thousands of poor Irish immigrants to settle on Indian land out West beyond Kansas. As an incentive, Gould not only offered the Irish protection, he also went public with promises that he would subsidize the settlers if they were in need of help. Displaced by the Irish Potato Famine, the first waves of Irish immigrants were happy to find fertile land and got along unexpectedly well with the local Indians. But problems had begun to arise when the railroad crews cut down more and more forestland, and water and local game seemed to vanish.

Joe arrived at the Paiute Reservation in the middle of a severe drought and invited the Paiute elders to his initial Ghost Dance. After ingesting *Toloache,* Joe shook with visions while performing an interpretation of Smohalla's ceremony. But the Paiute elders were unimpressed. After years of drought they were more interested in a rain dance. These old-timers knew that they were all about to become ghosts anyway, but they didn't want to be thirsty ones.

Fish Lake Joe realized that his last chance to get the Paiute elders' attention was to align his dance with Tavibo, their most renowned rainmaker. The legendary Tavibo had twice before brought the rain in a time of drought and had no reason to align himself with Fish Lake Joe, but that all changed when Joe predicted a terrible event.

THE LOCUST SIGN

Swarms of locusts appeared in the underworld, consuming vast parts of the Black Flower as they pelted the two halves of the ravaged ghost of the Toltec Ghost Dancer into a whirling frenzy. Fighting for composure and engulfed by a buzzing mass of vibrating wings, the left-hand half of the Toltec Ghost Dancer came up with a plan to drive the locusts out of the underworld. He quickly made a tool by tying a thin vine to a piece of flat wood and swung it in the air until it produced the same humming sound the locusts made when they rubbed their wings together in a swarm. This invention signaled the locusts to follow the sound and the Left-Hand Ghost Dancer led the insects to the edge of the petal where they seemed to disappear. The Left-Hand Ghost Dancer was proud of his developing skills, but his other half questioned his pride, realizing that what happened in the Black Flower below also reflected in the world above.

From out of the depths of the Black Flower, swarms of locusts appeared on the western prairies of the United States. Under every wilting cornstalk thousands of squirming locust larvae emerged and the stifling summer heat vibrated with the sound of the wings of millions of frenzied grasshoppers. This was the time of insects, when the actions of men drove nature out of balance and dreams were devoured.

Jay Gould, the robber baron behind the Union Pacific Railroad, was as far removed from nature as could be, a man who had never walked barefoot in nature. Gould had promised to subsidize and protect the homesteaders in times of need, but he ultimately failed to meet his obligation. All his decisions were based on one thing: how to make more money.

The homesteaders suffered under the swarm of the locust invasion for a year before the government finally responded. Washington's solution was the flamboyantly dressed ex-Civil War hero, Lieutenant George Armstrong Custer. However, Custer brought neither the promised provisions nor protection to the settlers. Instead, he introduced the pioneers to a new hope: the discovery of gold in the Black Hills of South Dakota.

Driven by hunger, the displaced homesteaders swarmed into the Black Hills like the locusts they had left behind. Unfortunately, the scared and starving settlers didn't realize that Custer was a political opportunist, purposely leading them out of an Indian frying pan and into an Indian fire because although there was very little gold to be found in the Black Hills, there was no shortage of angry Sioux Indians.

CHAPTER 12
THE SUNDANCE

The Locust Sign

D eath is but a reflection of life, a dream that cannot be remembered. And within the caverns of fear, the ghost of the Toltec Ghost Dancer had lost his faith. He suffered the great pain of hearing the cries of his loved ones from the world of the living without being able to aid them, while seeing ghosts of the Sioux people flooding into the underworld. His left-hand side yearned for his living descendants, but instead there was only more death as the ghosts of his relations danced around him.

MEN OF WAR

Shrouded ghosts of dead Sioux slowly danced around the Oval Office of the White House with their heads hung low. President Ulysses S. Grant took a double shot of bourbon and placed the glass on the table with a trembling hand. Though bourbon could temporarily stop the nightmares, the moment the effect of the alcohol wore off, the ghosts returned.

Ulysses S. Grant was a brilliant strategist who had led his country through a difficult time, but the killing fields of first the Civil War and then the Indian Wars drove him into a state of alcoholic depression. President Grant spent his last term in office drunk, painting beautiful oil paintings of the Indian people as if capturing their images would somehow end the tragedy he had brought down upon them.

Maintaining their culture more than many other tribes, the Sioux, Cheyenne and Arapaho peoples were buffalo hunters, and the eradication of the buffalo became the first step of General Sheridan's Final Solution. Within a few years, hired gunmen butchered the great herds of buffalo and antelope, reducing their numbers from a hundred million to a few thousand. Still, the Sioux followed their Hoop of Life, the migratory route of the Great Northern Herd of buffalo from the Yellowstone Mountains to the sacred Black Hills, determined to drive the invaders out. The Sioux, as a warrior society, were not interested in the peaceful Ghost Dance of the other tribes. They had their own ceremony: the Sundance.

The Sundance or *Wiwayak Wacipi* Prophecy began when the Sioux's beautiful female messiah, protected by a small white buffalo from the sacred herd called *Tehenshila*, stepped out of a snowstorm. White Buffalo Calf Woman gave the Sioux a sacred pipe called the *chunupa*, along with Seven Sacred Ceremonies that taught the Sioux how to become "true" human beings. The last of these ceremonies was the Sundance.

The Sioux did specific ceremonies, as they traveled the Hoop of Life, in the exact same manner as the Huichol. White Buffalo Calf Woman was also a manifestation of Precious Flower, the first Clean Sister who represented kindness, cleanliness, concern and love. Different terrain altered the lifestyle, but the ceremonies were one and the same. All the rituals of the Amerindian peoples, Northern and Southern, began with the first ritual: the Ghost Dance.

Before White Buffalo Calf Woman returned to her herd, she predicted the Tree of Life would pass through the winter of its own life. At that time, all the buffalo would vanish and the Sioux would suffer. After many seasons, when all hope was gone, the western winds of change would blow again and the missing herd of little buffalo, the *Tehenshila*, would return. From this herd, a sacred white buffalo would be born and White Buffalo Calf Woman would return to help heal a troubled land.

It was over one hundred and five degrees in the summer sun and the chokecherries were ripening. Sitting Bull was looking for a vision. He was the spiritual leader of his people, the Hunkpapa, one of the seven bands of the Lakota or Sioux. As White Buffalo Calf Woman had predicted, the buffalo were almost gone and the Sioux were suffering.

Like all Sundance ceremonies, this year's began with the cutting of a cottonwood tree. The tree was blessed by a maiden and became the center pole of the ceremony representing the Tree of Life. Eagle feathers, animal skulls, colored cloth and medicine bundles hung from the pole as offerings. At the center was the buffalo skull, the ultimate icon of the Sioux's rapidly vanishing way of life.

Sitting Bull wore nothing more than a horse blanket tied around his waist. He had a spotted eagle feather on each side of his head, tucked into a spruce-branch crown like rabbit ears. Hanging from his neck was a whistle made from the leg bone of an eagle. With a knife, he cut fifty-two slivers of flesh from each arm as a ceremonial offering of his commitment to the tribe through blood, just as the god *Quetzalcoatl* had once done to create humanity. In his other hand, Sitting Bull held a fan made from the wing of a golden eagle. He had already sweated, fasted, made offerings and sung for four days. Now cleansed, Sitting Bull was ready to dance the Sundance.

An old Hunkpapa medicine man took a long rope that hung from the top of the cottonwood pole and fastened it to Sitting Bull's chest. This rope was the symbol of the Sioux's Rope of the Dead. The old medicine man then secured the two split strands of the rope with slivers of buffalo bone pierced through both of Sitting Bull's pectoral muscles. Without flinching from the pain, Sitting Bull stared into the blazing sun and began to sing for all his relations, his relatives chanting with him in support. Sitting Bull then danced backward with little steps until the tethers pulled his flesh tight.

After four more days, staring into the blazing summer sun and still tied to the tethers, Sitting Bull finally stopped. Pulling the tethers through a notch in the top of the twenty-foot pole, two strong braves hoisted him into the air. His back arched as his flesh strained to hang on and not tear away from the bone slivers. Sitting Bull then blew the eagle bone whistle which made a high-pitched squeal.

As he dangled in the air, hanging from the Rope of the Dead, he danced with the ancestors, and just as his body went limp, his vision came. After the ceremony was complete, Sitting Bull healed from his chest wounds and held a council. Here he performed his tribal duty as medicine man by explaining what the ancestral ghosts had told him.

"I foresaw the tribes of the Great Plains coming together for a battle that will cost us a great price, but it is a battle which we will win. Soldiers will fall on our village like dead grasshoppers from the sky. We are not fighting for today or tomorrow. We are fighting for our children's children, Seven Generations from now."

President Grant drank alone, painting pictures of the vanishing Indian people, while Mrs. Julia Grant danced the waltz, tired of the oppressive weight of war. Mrs. Grant was intent on raising money to bring a bit of regal European refinement and charm to the White House.

In part, Julia Grant had financed her dream of creating an American royalty by receiving gifts for introducing the railroad tycoon, Jay Gould, to the man in control of the Indian Problem, General Sheridan. Together Sheridan and Gould had masterminded the first step of the Final Solution, the extermination of over 60,000,000 buffalo, the main food source of the tribes of the Great Plains.

President Grant was deeply angered over the situation and had placed General Armstrong Custer under house arrest for his part in the scandal. However, when the inebriated President Grant wasn't looking, the Secretary of War, William Tecumseh Sherman, Sheridan's political supporter in Washington, released Custer. In June 1876, without President Grant's knowledge,

Custer raced out West on the railroad to Chicago. Then he proceeded northwest, ignoring orders. He was anxious to achieve a huge, final victory over the united Great Plains tribes camped along the Little Bighorn River in Montana. Both Custer and the press were certain this battle would make him the next president of the United States.

THE PEACOCK AND THE SAGE

As Sitting Bull had seen in his vision, the Battle of the Little Bighorn ended in minutes. Custer's insatiable lust for killing women and children had betrayed him, leading him right into the trap set by Sitting Bull and Crazy Horse. Unfortunately for the Sioux, as Sitting Bull had predicted, this final victory was the beginning of the end. After the battle, Sitting Bull escaped to Canada while Crazy Horse stayed behind. Although Crazy Horse remained distant from the contemporaneous Ghost Dance Revival, he danced his own dance, linking himself with the ancestral ghosts by continuing to perform White Buffalo Calf Woman's Seven Sacred Ceremonies of the Sacred Pipe.

A year after the Battle of the Little Bighorn, embarrassed and fed up with his own mistakes, the presiding general of the Army, William Tecumseh Sherman, finally agreed with General Sheridan and called for the extermination of all hostile Indians not on reservations. Crazy Horse had evaded the troops for years, but after surrendering at Fort Robinson, Nebraska, he was eventually assassinated.

Over the next ten years, the momentarily united Nations of both the Southern and the Northern Great Plains were either killed or transferred to reservation lands. During this time, the starvation and disease on the reservations further ignited the Ghost Dance Revival. This revival soon reached a fevered pitch, spreading what little bit of hope was left from one reservation to the next.

CHAPTER 13
THE GHOST DANCE MESSIAHS

The Bat God (Piquete–Zina)

The two different sides of the Toltec Ghost Dancer walked together through petals of sorrow and, although they both cried for their loved ones, skeletons do not shed tears. Instead, the two halves of the same skeletal frame twisted in the darkness like a wounded beast. As the split skeleton suffered, the silhouettes of two men appeared. The first spoke to the right side of the Ghost Dancer and said that he was the Ghost Dance Messiah and only Jesus could mend the people's broken heart. Then the second spoke to the Ghost Dancer's left side in the voice of a plant and said that only the old ways could bring comfort to his people. Listening to these two ghostly voices, the different sides of the Toltec Ghost Dancer realized that his two sides had to choose which one would be sent to help the tribes and which side would remain to continue the journey below.

QUANAH PARKER

Long, black hair framed the copper face illuminated by a roaring fire inside a tipi where Quanah Parker, chief of the Comanche Nation, held a basket of peyote buttons, slowly praying before he chewed each one. When he had finished the last button he began to sing and fan the fire with an eagle feather fan, causing the smoke to rise. The fan guided the smoke over the body of a sick boy lying on the ground. Ghostly images of loved ones who had crossed over appeared in the smoke, and for a moment, Quanah could hear the voices of his ancestors speaking to him. The voices guided him to tap the boy on the forehead with a twig, leaving three tiny traces of healing pollen. When the boy finally awoke many hours later, he smiled and sat up, happy to be free of his sickness.

Quanah Parker, the Comanche chief, had learned how to speak to ghosts through peyote when he had become deathly ill as a child and was taken by his grandmother to a Tarahumara Indian healer in Mexico. The Tarahumara, first cousins of the Huichol, were experts in the use of peyote and Quanah learned how to heal directly from this sacrament of the Huichol Ghost Dance. Because the Comanche were confined to their reservation as prisoners of war, Quanah used peyote to keep his despondent tribe connected to its ancestral roots. Unfortunately, when the effects of the peyote wore off, the Comanche returned to the sorrow of reservation life.

WOVOKA

As the era of free-roaming Indians came to an end, Quanah Parker's peyote religion replaced the Ghost Dance as the most popular ceremony of the revival movement. Although the Ghost Dance had been at the heart of Indian resistance for centuries, it had failed to bring about the fulfillment of the Prophecy of Seven Generations. Peyote helped the tribes keep grounded in their indigenous roots, but the medicine did not fulfill the Seven Generations Prophecy, and so the suffering continued. From this despair, a final Ghost Dance Messiah arose who promised salvation and hope for the future. His name was Wovoka, or the Woodcutter.

The Walker River Paiute Reservation in Nevada was bitterly cold on New Year's Day of 1889, but the sun was out. Wrapped in a blanket, Wovoka, the orphaned son of the rainmaker Tavibo, ghost danced around a buffalo skull altar singing, "Christian God, come and relieve the Indian people's suffering. Show us a sign so we can carry on in this terrible time."

Suddenly, the moon began to move across the sun and finally it blocked out all the light in a full solar eclipse. A crowd of spectators began to form, transfixed as they watched day turn into night. Wovoka continued to dance and chant. "Grandfather, I ask you to give us back the light so this world can be born again."

As the sunlight returned from behind the moon, the crowd exhaled a sigh of relief. Then Wovoka fell to the ground in a fevered trance. No longer skeptical, the Paiute listened attentively as Wovoka sat up and began interpreting his vision.

"I have traveled to the place of the ancestral ghosts and have brought this dust back from their land as proof." With his eyes glazed over in trance, Wovoka opened his palm and showed the expanding crowd the strange gray dust.

"Seven Generations is here and soon the One God will roll up the earth, destroying all the mines, towns and farm animals of the foreigners who have fouled the integrity of our beloved Mother. Ghost Dancers will survive because the Holy Ghost will lift them up into the tallest trees high above the ground, and then a great flood will cleanse this land. When the waters recede, the Ghost Dancers that followed the Holy Ghost will be placed back on the ground. I am an Indian but have become the reincarnation of Jesus Christ and have been sent by the One God to prepare his Lost Tribe, the Indian people."

Then Wovoka instructed his followers, "Be good Indians and do not resist or cause any trouble. All you have to do is keep ghost dancing and the One God, my Father, will do the rest. Our dead ancestors will live again."

The event was powerful and many of those who attended believed that they saw Wovoka perform miracles, including levitation and raising the ghosts of the dead. Overnight, Wovoka's promise to fulfill the Prophecy of Seven Generations spread like brushfire on a windswept plain and many came to the Walker River Indian Reservation to learn his version of the *Natdia*, or Ghost Dance. But as fate would have it, Wovoka would not be the one to dance the last dance.

KICKING BEAR

Returning to the Standing Rock Reservation after ghost dancing with Wovoka, a Oglala Sioux holy man, Kicking Bear, went to pay his respects to a Hunkpapa holy man, Sitting Bull. Kicking Bear told Sitting Bull he believed that the time of salvation had finally arrived.

"Uncle, while you were away in Canada, I went to ghost dance with Wovoka and saw with my own eyes the miracles others speak of. I truly believe Wovoka is the Messiah and the time of the Prophecy of Seven Generations is here. If you ghost dance with me, others will follow. "

Sitting Bull refused. "For seasons upon seasons, I have been the head of the Seven Fires' Ghost Society and have communed with the ancestral ghosts. I do not believe that this kind of missionary round dance can bring dead loved ones back to the flesh as the Paiute Ghost Dance prophet Wovoka preaches. That is the talk of the bible flippers, but if it brings hope to the people, I have no problem with this dance."

On a freezing-cold November day, during one of the harshest winters in history, Kicking Bear decided to ghost dance without Sitting Bull. Barely hidden behind a row of frost-covered trees, nearly thirty Sioux had gathered to ghost dance at Standing Rock.

After crawling out of an *inipi* sweat lodge, Kicking Bear put on a ghost dance shirt with symbols of crescent moons, five-pointed stars and mythical animals drawn upon the cheap reservation cloth. His head held low, he walked towards the dancers who were wrapped in tattered blankets like wind-torn scarecrows on an Arctic landscape. Their grieving faces were painted red with a black half-moon on the cheek or forehead.

As Kicking Bear entered the circle, a dancer pulled a prohibited Colt revolver out from under his filthy blanket and shot Kicking Bear at close range, but he did not fall. Instead, Kicking Bear's voice rose up to a dramatic pitch as he exclaimed, "This ghost dance shirt has the power to protect us from the bluecoat's bullets. We now have the power to protect ourselves."

The Ghost Dancers answered with an eerie cry. "Father, give us back our arrows, give us back our arrows."

Then they washed themselves head to foot with handfuls of Mother Earth to remove the stench of the "civilized world."

Kicking Bear raised his sacred pipe to the four directions and the dancers fell silent. Then Kicking Bear began to speak.

"The missionaries claim that the Indian people are being punished because our ancestors belonged to the Lost Tribe that killed Jesus Christ. I say that this is a lie. The Indians did not kill the beloved Jesus. The white man did and framed the Indians to cover up their crime. To right this wrong and stop the white man's lies and destruction, Grandfather *Thunkashila* has sent us Jesus in the body of Wovoka, an Indian dressed as a white man. Wovoka is our Messiah."

The dancers then took each other's hands and began dancing counterclockwise in a large circle. They picked up momentum, moving faster and faster, spinning with what little strength they had until the circle disintegrated and the dancers broke ranks, leaping about, dancing wildly with invisible partners or falling to the frozen ground and shaking, lost in a quivering trance.

Hidden from sight on the other side of the cottonwoods, the Indian agent James McLaughlin and his wife watched the spectacle through binoculars. Mrs. McLaughlin began to tremble and grow faint, believing she had seen demonic ghosts dancing with crazed savages. McLaughlin saw something else, an opportunity to cover up his theft and black market resale of the Sioux's food rations. In an attempt to hide his deceit, McLaughlin sent a telegram to Washington, claiming that the Sioux version of the Ghost Dance was being used to incite violence and that his wife feared for her life. McLaughlin demanded that the government end the Ghost Dance ceremonies at Standing Rock.

Washington ignored McLaughlin's requests for months, until desperate, McLaughlin made false accusations that Sitting Bull was behind the sudden popularity of the ceremony. Since the military still held a grudge against Sitting Bull for defeating them at the Battle of the Little Bighorn, they saw McLaughlin's petition as an opportunity to settle the score.

Targeting Sitting Bull while ignoring both Kicking Bear and Wovoka, the US government outlawed the Ghost Dance and issued a warrant for the great chief's arrest. That night, Sitting Bull could not sleep and began to sing his ghost song. "Grandfather *Thunkashila*, through you my ancestors may hear me and I say to them, if we cannot live as who we are then today is a good day to die."

The next morning, a frigid Christmas Eve, reservation police sent by Agent McLaughlin burst into Sitting Bull's cabin and arrested him for using the now-illegal Ghost Dance to promote insurgency. During the arrest, a struggle ensued and Sitting Bull was murdered. The chain of events that began with Wovoka teaching Kicking Bear to ghost dance and ending with Sitting Bull's death signaled the end of the Ghost Dance Revival and set the stage for the 1890 massacre at Wounded Knee.

With Sitting Bull, the last symbol of Indian resistance, dead, the government was anxious to end the Indian Wars. They purposely sent Custer's 7th Cavalry to intercept Chief Blackfoot, Sitting Bull's cousin, and his band of Hunkpapa Sioux near Wounded Knee Creek. Mostly women and children, the group had come to Wounded Knee Creek so the widows could ghost dance one last time as free Indians and see their dead loved ones before they turned themselves in at the reservation death camps.

As the Indians were being herded together, the cavalry positioned heavy artillery on a mound above the creek. Unable to hear what was going on, a deaf Hunkpapa man resisted and pulled an old rifle from under his tattered blanket. In response, the cavalry opened fire on the unarmed Indians. Minutes later, the smoke cleared and the US 7th Cavalry believed they had just exterminated the last free-roaming band of American Indians. This was the Final Solution, ending with the last military action of one of the largest genocides in history.

On that small mound at Wounded Knee, South Dakota, in 1890, history's era of wild and free American Indians ended. The Ghost Dance Revival had failed and with it the hope that the indigenous people could return to their traditional niche in the tapestry of life. Though it seemed that all hope was lost, deep in the heart of the earth, a Toltec Ghost Dancer was keeping the beat of the sacred dance alive. And soon his earthly counterpart would rise up from the soil and dance the dance once more.

CHAPTER 14
THE CRIMSON JESTER

The Banner of Zapata's Army

As *Tezcatlipoca's* dark shadow of night shrouded the Indian people's day, the Toltec Ghost Dancer continued to dance, following the steps of the American Grail through the Black Flower below. In the distance, the Ghost Dancer could hear the thundering hoofs of the souls of millions of exterminated buffalo entering the underworld and turning to bones. Enraged by the slaughter, *Chicón Tokosho*, the Lord of the Mountain, let out a deafening rumble that reverberated down through the underworld, causing subterranean mountains to collide.

Struggling to keep his balance on trembling ground, the right side of the Toltec Ghost Dancer slipped into a crack in the belly of the beast, but his left side pulled him from the crevice. Reunited, his two sides then entered the next petal of the Black Flower, the home of the jaguar god *Tepeyollotl*. *Tepeyollotl* was associated with *Tezcatlipoca*, the Lord of Witches and the Lord of Days. This jaguar god, *Tepeyollotl*, ate the flesh of the living and his roar caused earthquakes that shattered illusions.

The Ghost Dancer watched as the gigantic jaguar slowly slunk out of a cave. Holding his ground, the Toltec Ghost Dancer made a stand and raised three of the pieces of the *tiponi*, the carved jaguar bones. The jaguar god roared, "Who is this that defiles my sanctuary with the bones of my ancestor?"

The Ghost Dancer answered, "It is I, the Ghost Dancer, and I have come to learn the gift of your strength so my generations may live."

Instead of pouncing on the Toltec's skeletal bones, the jaguar god pulled back his claws and decided to teach the Ghost Dancer what he needed to know to mend the Rope of the Dead. As the giant jaguar shook himself all over, the black spots of his yellow coat burst into a million mosquitoes. Then the mosquitoes swarmed the Ghost Dancer, who slapped at the biting demons. The flying horde almost drove the Toltec crazy, but he managed to find a deep inner strength which allowed him to calmly walk out of the black cloud. Once he had moved beyond the swarm, the Toltec turned south, walking towards the place where the Ghost Dance had first begun so long ago. As he walked, he started to see the outlines of a dancing ghost rise up from out of the underworld.

CATALUNYA

In 1882, Julián Díaz-Ordaz, a Spaniard, purchased hundreds of acres of the Sierra Mazatecan cloud forest from the Mexican government to build a coffee plantation. He hired local Indians to cut back the cloud forest, build a hacienda he named Catalunya and plant his seeds. Some of the locals were happy to get the work, while others felt resentful of the Spaniard's incursion onto their land. Unbeknownst to Ordaz, he had purchased some of the most sacred soil of the Americas.

Barefoot and wearing the traditional woven *serape* of the Mazatec tribe, twenty-year-old José Martínez stood on a cliff above the village of Agua de Pozol and looked down upon Rancho Catalunya. Julían Ordaz had cut the cloud forest back to the very place where the bearded Stranger had first ghost danced. With a fixed stare José watched as the second stranger to ever enter the region cut down acres of cedar trees, and José wondered why the Lord of the Mountain had allowed this Spaniard to defile consecrated ground.

To answer his own questions, José Martínez decided to seek the counsel of the ancestors. José left his perch and walked down a hidden path that led him to a forest where he began to collect the flesh-like, phallic mushrooms called the Little Ones. After collecting the Little Ones, Martínez and his young wife, a Clean Sister, crawled into a small hole covered by foliage in the side of the mountain above Agua de Pozol. There, a tiny cave opened up into a larger chamber with a small, milky-white pool of water at its center. Along the walls, ancient pottery was stacked, and at the rear of the cave, a skeleton rested. The strings that once held the skeleton's ornaments together were long gone, but his earthly treasures of gold and beads still lay all around him. This was the cave of *Huehueteotl*, Grandfather Fire.

By the white pool, José ate the Little Ones while his wife lit a candle, then he addressed the crest of the candle's flame. "Grandfather Fire, I wish to ask *Chicón Nindo*, the Lord of this Mountain, why he is allowing his sacred land to be defiled by an outsider."

José's wife put out the candle with a bell-capped flower while José rested on a straw mat. Half an hour later, a distant wind could be heard rushing through the leaves on the trees and picking up momentum as it raced toward the cave. Lightning cracked across the sky and thunder rumbled, rolling through the dark clouds. Racing down the path on a black stallion, a mustachioed stranger with a large, white sombrero flew by like the wind. Inside their thatched huts, the local families huddled together in the dark and whispered the name of *Chicón Nindo*, the Lord of their Mountain. The wind passed, the night grew still and José's young wife relit the candle.

In the wink of an eye, a flickering glimpse of a presence entered the cave and moved through the shadows shyly. After a moment's hesitation, an earnest voice spoke softly from the shadows. At first the voice spoke in a tongue even older than Mazatec, but then it repeated its words in a language José could understand. "I am only a voice crying out from the wilderness, but the past, present and future are all mine to see."

The voice paused and the forest was silent, then the voice spoke again. "You will live to be a very old man, José, and then you will tie the final knot of this Reed Cycle's Ghost Dance with the ritual you have begun tonight."

In awe of the imposing presence, José and his young wife could not lift their heads to look as the voice continued to speak. "These words I speak will come to pass, for I have already seen what will be. By the time this knot is tied, the Long Night of the Indian people will reach a climax as the ice on the top of the world melts. The trees will have fallen and the birds will have vanished from the great Jungle of the South. This will be the time when the bees lose their gift of flight and the frogs can no longer sing. This is when the final battle for the Fifth World will begin."

José listened attentively so he could hear every word.

"As sure as the sun will rise, soon the wild and free spirit of the Plumed Serpent will also rise up from this land in the body of a man who will send this foreigner, Julían Ordaz, flying like tufted seeds in the wind, spreading the word of what he has seen. As part of the Lord of the Mountain's plan to save the Fifth World, this man will plant the ideas of Precious Flower in the minds of the conqueror's children. Mother Nature's heart will keep the beat and I will call the steps, but it is you, José, who will orchestrate the Ghost Dance. Now, tie your first knot."

Distant thunder rumbled and the words of *Desheto* were like a whispering wind that arrives in a gust but is gone a moment later. José Martínez tied a symbolic knot from a swirling strand of smoke which then rose up from the burning copal incense as he chanted: "*Sequah eh, ah eh oh, ah eh, ah eh, ah eh oh.*"

Lightning crackled and thunder rumbled across the sky. As the frogs began to sing, the rains came. The Ghost Dancer José Martínez was a rainmaker and he knew that the ritual was now complete. He had only to wait for it to manifest in the world.

SPIRIT IN THE FLESH

During the spring of 1905, fifteen years after the Ghost Dance massacre at Wounded Knee, the Spirit of the Americas once again rose up from the soil of its origin in the form of a man. Under a foreboding sky, the Crimson Jester, Emiliano Zapata, a lean, mustachioed Indian medicine man, danced and prayed for a vision at the cave of the Aztec goddess *Coyolxauhqui. Coyolxauhqui* was the moon goddess related to the coyote, betrayal and the reincarnation of the dead. While the modern world wrote them off, the ancestral ghosts, the Clean Sisters, the Ghost Dancers and the plants were waging a hidden struggle to restore the Tree of Life.

At the cave of the coyote, Zapata was initiated by his spiritual mentor Tobat Ko, the ancestral high priest of the Huichol Indians. Just like Quanah Parker, the Huichol had eaten the top buttons of the peyote cactus and communed with ancestors through the sacrament of plants. Encircled by the smoke of copal incense, Emiliano Zapata's vision soon appeared and his mission became clear. Zapata would become the living manifestation of the indomitable wild and free spirit of the land: the Plumed Serpent.

Defying all prejudice, the mustachioed Zapata rose to power and soon drove all of the European landowners out of southern Mexico. With his victories, Zapata did the unimaginable: he united the tribes south of Mexico City into the first free Indian nation since the conquest. The Western media branded him a *bandito* because they had neither words for nor understanding of who he really was.

Zapata's banner was the Virgin of Guadalupe standing upon a skull and cross bones, symbolizing the Aztec goddess *Tonantzin*. Through Zapata, even Guadalupe was returning to her indigenous roots. Though the Ghost Dance of the United States had been obliterated, its spirit was still very much alive south of the border.

With a twist that was typically Mexican, the Crimson Jester raised the Ghost Dance from the grave by establishing the *Día de Muertos*, the Day of the Dead, as the official holiday of the Mexican Revolution. On the first of November, barefoot peasants joyously paraded around plazas once off limits to those too poor to own shoes. Candy skulls, still secretly representing the real ones used in the Aztecs' Lady of the Dead ceremony, decorated the plazas. The intoxicated peasants danced, wearing the costumes of skeletons dressed like Zapata's dead comrades.

After twilight, the people would leave the plaza and visit the gravesites of their beloved relatives. Like the Aztec at the Lady of the Dead ceremonies, the people placed marigold flowers on the graves along with food and drink for their dead. They would drink, sing and dance until just after midnight, when the ghosts of their beloved relatives would joyfully rise from the grave and dance with them till dawn. As soon as the *Día de Muertos* was over, the *Zapatistas* and their women returned to the battlefield. Now protected by their ancestral ghosts, these humble Indians began to take Mexico back from the Spanish.

To drown out the sorrows of war, the Spaniards had planted sugarcane and distilled the liquid into alcohol that both sides of the conflict consumed as fast as the firewater could be processed. Crude sugarcane rum called *aguardiente* became the sacrament of the Day of the Dead, but water was not the only thing that was on fire in Mexico.

Zapata burned down the plantations so they would go feral and the *indios* could once again live off of the land. These burning haciendas became the flames of the largest and most successful Indian revolution in American history. Twenty-five years after Wounded Knee, the Indian Wars were not over and neither was the Ghost Dance. The wars and the dance had simply moved south, returning to the land of their origin. Zapata, the Crimson Jester, had reunited the tribes once more and had succeeded in taking control of half of Mexico.

Far away in New York City, the robber barons who had made their fortunes stealing land and resources from the Indians were not happy. The Crimson Jester's indigenous revolution was driving wealthy foreigners out of southern Mexico and threatening Wall Street's business interests in Mexico. As clouds of cigar smoke rose above the Wall Street boardroom where the economic lords of the United States discussed the fate of Zapata, the wealthy elite came to a decision. The robber barons gave the revolutionary government of Mexico a choice: get rid of Zapata and his Indian army or be crushed with an iron fist.

Sitting at a small café in the port of Veracruz, the Crimson Jester, disguised as a poor *indio*, watched as the US Marines landed their mammoth warships. At that moment, Zapata realized the entire revolution would be crushed if he and his indigenous army continued to resist the US invasion. The revolution had to be turned over to the peasant populace if it had any hope of survival. Returning home to Morelos, Zapata began his last Ghost Dance as a human, first saying goodbye to his indigenous Otomi wife, a Clean Sister, before heading out to meet his destiny. Upon his black stallion named Lightning, Zapata purposely rode right into the trap the US Army had paid Venustiano Carranza, *Primer Jefe* of the revolutionary Mexican Constitutionalist Army, to set for him.

Zapata's head was taken as if it were still the time of the Aztec and his body was hung on display in a plaza. In true Toltec Ghost Dance fashion, Zapata had sacrificed himself for the greater good of the tribe. But it was through Zapata's ceremonial suicide in the shadow of the Plumed Serpent that the Mexican people survived.

CHAPTER 15
TALKING PLANTS

The Voice of the Little Ones

Carried by the vulture spirit, the bones of Emiliano Zapata were brought to rest in the heart of the Black Flower. At the same moment the vulture touched down, the Toltec Ghost Dancer arrived at the petal of the Black Flower where the spirits of plants rest before they bloom again. There he saw the hallowed deer *Kauyumari*, the spirit animal of peyote, playing among the sacred cacti.

The Lord of Witches had been stalking the Toltec for centuries and now saw the Ghost Dancer enter the Petal of Eternal Spring. When the god saw the Ghost Dancer and *Kauyumari* together, he knew he had to end their meeting. So he drew his bow and shot an arrow, wounding the sacred deer. The Ghost Dancer felt as if the arrow had also pierced his own heart and knew that if the *nagual* of peyote, *Kauyumari*, died, the visionary plant would no longer have a spirit guide to give direction to his wounded descendants in the world of the living.

THE GENIE IN THE BOTTLE

In 1919, almost twenty-nine years after the Ghost Dance ended at Wounded Knee, an Austrian scientist named Ernst Spath synthesized mescaline from the Huichol's peyote cactus. With this discovery a sacrament of the Ghost Dance was accidently released upon the world like a genie from a bottle, and within ten years, mescaline had become all the rage in Berlin. Herman Hesse's classic novel *Steppenwolf* was based on this mind-expanding movement when ancient sacraments were first synthesized into their chemical components and the derivatives used recreationally or for self-realization.

While Europe was falling under the spell of mescaline, Zapata's army was busy driving out the Europeans living in Mexico. In the Sierra Mazateca, Julián Díaz-Ordaz ran for his life as Zapata's fire-wielding General Panuncio Martínez came to burn down Rancho Catalunya. Deported from the port of Veracruz, Ordaz returned to Spain, carrying with him the first stolen artifacts and stories of the ancient pre-Columbian Mushroom Cult based on the Ghost Dance. To the Spanish upper class, these objects and beliefs were just the peculiarities of a primitive people, so Ordaz decided to take the artifacts to Berlin where he believed they would be more fully appreciated.

Instead, German archaeologists refuted Ordaz's story, believing that he had misinterpreted the images inscribed on his artifacts and confused a mushroom for a peyote button. Disillusioned, Ordaz returned to Spain, not realizing that he had planted the seed of the Ghost Dance and its sacred mushroom in the tainted soil of the Modern Age.

In December of 1936, a small bi-plane flew over the tropical cloud forest of the Sierra Mazateca, the birthplace of the Ghost Dance and the home of the Little Ones. The forest Indians who watched from below cowered in fear at the sight of the plane's fuselage and wings, mistaking the craft for the Cross of Christ that the Catholic *padres* had told them would come from heaven at the world's end.

Though the world survived the plane's approach, the Mazatecan's understanding of their world was about to transform forever. As quickly as the plane appeared in the sky, it vanished again over the mountaintops and landed on the other side of the mountain near the hamlet of Huautla de Jiménez.

With concerned faces, the bronze-skinned Indians watched as two young American women, a bald Mexican pilot and an American man carrying a heavy metal case emerged from the interior of the plane. The Catholic priest from Huautla greeted the strangers warmly and asked about their mission in the region.

One of the women, Eunice Pike, told the priest she was a translator from the Summer Institute of Linguistics in the United States and was in Mexico to record the Mazatec language for science. Though the priest took her at her word, he wondered why Eunice Pike had chosen the Mazatec and Huautla out of all the tens of thousands of remote pueblos in Mexico. Was it just happenstance or had the translator known beforehand about the mysterious pre-Columbian practices of the region?

When Pike wasn't translating she wrote many essays about the Mazatec religion, witchcraft and rituals. After reading Pike's impressions, her secret benefactors, the Wycliffe Bible Translators, told her to find out more about the "poison mushroom" the Mazatecans used in their rituals and the plumed beast they were rumored to worship. Pike found this task difficult because the Indians believed these mushrooms were so sacred they never spoke about them. As for the beast, all the Indians would say was that the creature used to live in the forest on the other side of the mountain. But finally, after years of asking, Pike was invited to watch a candle ritual called a *velada*.

Visiting-anthropologist Robert Weitlaner and his daughter were present at the ceremony, although they remained spectators. Pike herself, even though she did not eat the Little Ones, left the *velada* believing that the devil had revealed himself to her as the Beast of the Apocalypse, and that this red dragon was also the Mazatecan's Plumed Serpent. The local Catholic priests supported Pike's theory, explaining that the natives believed that the poison mushrooms the witches ate grew from the spilled blood of this beast.

Pike sent a telegram to her Wycliffe connection, William Cameron Townsend, letting him know she had found what he had been looking for. In turn, Townsend, the founder of Wycliffe Bible Translators, contacted the Office of Strategic Services or OSS, which would later became the CIA. The OSS began researching the possible military uses of mind-altering plants. The OSS then sent Dr. Richard Evans Schultes, an ethnobiologist from Harvard, to investigate the situation.

When Schultes arrived in Huautla, Pike arranged for him to witness a Mazatecan mushroom *velada*. Before dusk, Schultes was taken to a hidden basement in an adobe house where an altar lit with candles was set up against a stained, white wall. Schultes watched as the healer and her patient both ate six pairs of mushrooms. Then the candle was blown out and the healer began to sing. Even though Schultes did not ingest the mushroom sacrament during the ritual, he sensed an unseen presence in the room. Excited by his experience, Schultes returned to the US and shared his experience with the OSS, corroborating Eunice Pike's claim that a pre-Columbian religion based on the sacred mushroom still existed in Huautla.

During World War II, the CIA discontinued their "poison mushroom" research and Schultes did not return to the Mazateca until the war was over. In the interim, Schultes visited one of the world's preeminent authorities on mushrooms, R. Gordon Wasson. Wasson, who was also a vice president of J.P. Morgan & Co., grew excited when he heard the story of the *velada* and showed Schultes an illustration from an ancient version of the Bible. This Bible depicted the Fruit of Knowledge as a mushroom. Based upon this detailed illustration as well as his own mycological research, Wasson had come up with a theory: he believed that a mind-altering mushroom was the Fruit of Knowledge and had given human beings their first religious experiences.

To prove this theory, Wasson made the arduous journey to Huautla in 1955 where he met a Mazatec Indian healer named María Sabina. Through translators Sabina told Wasson, "I have foreseen your arrival in a dream. The Virgin Mother has told me to perform a *velada* to help heal your broken heart."

Wasson was shocked because Sabina had spoken the truth about something she could not have known. He had been heartbroken ever since the death of his beloved mother just months before he traveled to Mexico. Even though Wasson had promised his wife that he would not eat the strange mushrooms he had come to research, Wasson could not resist the intrigue of the healer's inexplicable insight.

The evening of the ceremony, Wasson was taken to a tiny adobe house and led to the basement where he was instructed to sit upon a straw *petate* mat on the floor. In the windowless room Sabina lit a single beeswax candle and whispered in Mazatec as she passed the fleshy mushrooms in pairs through the copal incense smoke and then offered them to Wasson.

After ingesting the Little Ones, Wasson lay down along with his companions as Sabina began to first chant and then sing. With each melodic phrase, Wasson's fears faded into an inner warmth, and as he dissolved into this warmth, a startlingly clear image of his deceased mother appeared from the darkness and spoke to him, telling him how happy she was to see him again. Wasson, a conservative Republican banker from New York City, had communed with the ghost of his mother.

Coming down from this otherworldly experience, Wasson racked his mind to figure out what had really happened. The more he thought, the more he kept coming back to the same puzzling question. Wasson believed in Darwin's theory that every property in nature was designed for a specific survival-related purpose. "So why," wondered Wasson, "had these mushrooms developed an ability to affect the human mind in such a way?"

The Mazatecans viewed the mushroom somewhat differently, believing that plants communicated with each other and that these specific mushrooms, called the Little Ones, allowed humans to tap into an underground network of plant communication.

Still seeking answers, Wasson began to research the few remaining codex journals of the Aztec and Mixtec peoples, carefully scrutinizing their ancient texts in the belief that the ancient Mesoamericans must have known of the Little Ones' existence.

Viewing the Mixtec codices through new eyes, Wasson found illustrations he was certain depicted mushroom ceremonies. He also found the name the Aztec had given the sacred mushroom: *Teonanacatl*, or the Astonishing Gift of the Gods.

As Wasson dug deeper into this ancient mystery, Schultes, in his role as a government liaison, arranged a meeting between Wasson and the CIA. The agents asked the reluctant Wasson to help them collect sacred mushrooms to be tested for possible military purposes. Wasson was a staunch supporter of the US military, but had been so moved by his experience that he felt it would be blasphemous to use the sacred mushrooms for any form of mind control or violence. Caught up in a spiritual quagmire, he decided that the only way to protect the Fruit of Knowledge from a violent fate was to introduce it to the world at large.

A few months after Wasson's meeting with the CIA, the fantastic tale of María Sabina, a modern-day witch who could commune with ghosts through a sacred mushroom, appeared as a feature article in *Life* magazine. For most readers, this was nothing more than a curious tale from an exotic land, completely beyond the limits of their understanding, but the article was about to change modern civilization forever and bring the Ghost Dance back from the grave.

CHAPTER 16
THE LORD OF THE MOUNTAIN

The Mushroom Practitioner

For *Tezcatlipoca*, who had returned from hunting in the underworld, the insult was unbearable. "How could my brother, the Plumed Serpent, give the Fruit of Knowledge to the human parasites after I, a god, have been refused it?" To add injury to insult, even *Kauyumari*, the peyote deer, had survived the Lord of Witches' poison arrow.

Up until now, *Quetzalcoatl's* magical work had been seamless. From María Sabina to Eunice Pike, then Richard Schultes, R. Gordon Wasson and finally *Life* magazine, the Plumed Serpent's seed of knowledge, the sacrament of his Ghost Dance, had been carried across time and into the Modern Age. Not only did the sacred mushrooms tear the illusion of reality, they were about to make history.

But now, a human was needed to manifest the Prophecy of Seven Generations. So the Toltec Ghost Dancer, deep in the bowels of the earth, began to dance a Pied Piper into existence, one that would lead the Ghost Dance into the Modern Age.

THE PIED PIPER

At the Human Be-In in 1967, Timothy Leary calmly instructed the youth of America to "turn on, tune in, drop out" using a mind-expanding drug called LSD. Frustrated with the establishment, the youth of America eagerly followed this "Pied Piper" on a chemically induced trip into another reality.

This "pied piper's" Ghost Dance journey had begun seven years earlier when he came to lecture at Harvard about the possibility of curing mental illness with pharmaceutical drugs. Leary was among a group of young scientists who were beginning to think outside the box and question both the possibilities and limits of chemicals and consciousness.

When Leary read Wasson's article about María Sabina in *Life* magazine, he became so intrigued by the possibilities of using the psilocybin alkaloid in the "magic mushrooms" to cure mental illness that he immediately left for southern Mexico.

Unlike Wasson, Leary was not interested in what he saw as the Mazatecan's primitive superstitions, so he ate a different species of the magic mushrooms without the *velada* ritual. Consequently, his vision was more of a personal journey through his own mind, rather than a healing ceremony or an encounter with ancestral ghosts. Even so, Leary's extraordinary mushroom experience altered his consciousness in ways he could not have imagined at the time. Inspired by this psychotropic awakening, Leary co-wrote *The Psychedelic Experience*, based on the *Tibetan Book of the Dead*, and ushered in the mind-expanding 1960s.

Convinced that his experience had been chemically induced rather than spiritual in nature, Leary began taking large doses of both psilocybin, an isolated alkaloid of the mushroom, and LSD, a powerful psychedelic synthesized from another type of fungus. His hope was that the more powerful the dose, the more profound the experience would be. Filled with the bravado that he had discovered God in pill form, Leary became the pied piper who unknowingly led the youth of America right to the Ghost Dance.

Turned on by the twinkle in the eye of this pied piper, celebrities and international rock stars showed up in Huautla. These famous youth icons were searching for a more natural connection to the psychedelic experiences that had taken over the sub-culture of their generation. But before the rock gods ever caught a glimpse of what Wasson had experienced, the austerity of the dirt-poor Mazatecan's harsh lifestyle drove them from the mountain.

Nevertheless, the tear in *Tezcatlipoca's* Veil of Illusion had opened into a small hole and the hippies soon flooded into Huautla on the heels of the famous trendsetters, eager to "trip" with María Sabina. But these young thrill seekers had no idea they had just stumbled into the middle of a ritual that had begun thousands of years earlier.

The locals of Huautla knew nothing about *Life* magazine, psychedelic drugs or the Western concept of mind expansion, so they couldn't understand why these strange outsiders came to

María Sabina's shack asking her for magic mushrooms. The people of Huautla couldn't even figure out how the foreigners had found out about their sacrament, since the Little Ones were so sacred, even members of the same family never spoke to each other about them, never mind to outsiders. Feeling that María Sabina had broken their deepest taboo, her own tribe branded her a pariah.

To address the mounting culture clash, Julieta, a respected healer, was sent by the municipal president Isauro Nava García to the cave of the people's ancient patron god, *Chicón Tokosho*, Mazatec for the Lord of Days or *Tezcatlipoca*. Julieta was told to find out what the god had to say about the hippie invasion of Huautla and their use of the Little Ones. The *presidente* of the pueblo thought that because the Mazatecan's Lord of Days was a god of wealth and commerce, he might help the poor Indians by giving his blessing to the sale of the sacred Little Ones. After all, if the god had not punished María Sabina, why couldn't others profit from the mushroom as well?

Chicón Tokosho lived alone in a cave on a barren mountain above Huautla. Nothing grew outside the cave because wherever the god was strong, nature died, though it was believed that he could bring wealth as a patron.

Julieta entered the cave, lit her candle and ate the Little Ones. Half an hour later, her vision began when *Chicón Tokosho* appeared as a giant snake curled around a shimmering tabernacle. Like a Catholic priest, *Chicón Tokosho* lived alone without a woman, but he accepted the Clean Sister's offering of *cacao* and allowed her to sit on his fleshy lap like a chair. Julieta spoke to the god with the most humble inflection.

"Oh Great Lord of the Mountain, I have been sent by the pueblo for your counsel. Strangers called hippies have come from a faraway land and they somehow know of the Little Ones."

The Lord of the Mountain answered, "No one comes to this mountain on their own accord; they can only be brought. María Sabina has done the bidding of our Ghost Dancer, the Old Turtle, and has brought these foreigners."

"Oh Great Lord, these foreigners are very rich, but have only come to buy the Little Ones. We are so poor and hungry! Would you, a god of commerce, grant us permission to sell the more common variety of Little Birds for a few *toshsquah* trade shells worth of *pesos* if this would not interfere with the Old Turtle's dance?"

Hissing with his darting tongue, *Chicón Tokosho* answered, "Hear me clearly: turkey-neck disease will fall upon all those that sell any of the Little Ones. Earn your trade shells by selling them the mushrooms of white man's saints that grow in the cow dung and sugar cane fields that the white man brought to us. Those cow dung mushrooms are there to hide the truly sacred Little Ones."

When Julieta returned to the pueblo of Huautla, she told the local authorities *Chicón Tokosho* had said they could sell the cow pie and sugar cane mushrooms but never the Little Ones. Because these mushrooms were much more abundant, their usage quickly spread among the hordes of young foreigners now flooding into Huautla. Without a ritual to guide them, the hippies ate the magic mushrooms of white men's saints. But caught up in their freestyle "Be-In," some hippies had bad trips, and one even bit off a live chicken's head in the town square. The crazier things became, the more afraid and offended the locals grew. In response, the bad apples in the local community began to rob the tripping foreigners of their money and possessions.

Attempting to escape scary "bad vibes," the rain-soaked hippies flooded out of Huautla and ended up camping under the Puente de Fierro, a metal bridge just below the pueblo.

Unbeknownst to the hippies, the Mazatecan god of lust, *Chato*, lived in a cave under this same bridge. Struggling to make sense of the situation, the locals came up with their own theory: the poorer hippies had come to eat the white man's saints and make offerings to *Chato*, so they could get rich like the rock stars who had come before them.

Chato was half man and half tawny goat, the god of lust and the keeper of the sexual power of magic. He was the giver of wealth, but also the gatekeeper for the gods of nature. The Mazatecans believed that if you ate the white saints' mushrooms and brought offerings to *Chato's* cave, you could ask for material wealth, but *Chato's* blessing had a price.

After asking *Chato's* favor, the next time you ate the white saints' mushrooms, the god would arrive late at night when you were sleeping and sniff you up and down. *Chato* would then violate you, *Ah lat sah*, "snake-in-hole." Whether you were a woman or a man, it did not matter. Then he would mark you. After your wealth came, his mark would also be upon one of your children as a birth defect.

Chato was not a god of the old pantheon; he had arrived at the same time as the Catholic priests. But he had become the gatekeeper who kept outsiders from discovering the true secret hidden on the other side of the mountain.

To deflect the hippies' attention away from the ancient mystery just beyond their view, *Chato* turned the hippie refugee camp under the bridge into a mushroom-induced orgy. Tales of murderous *banditos* on the other side of the mountain also kept the foreign invaders from venturing further.

Even though the young hippie pilgrims had come very close, they still had no idea *Chato* had purposely stopped them at the edge of an ancient twilight zone: the place where the Ghost Dance had once begun.

The metal bridge where the hippies and *Chato* met crossed a river gorge which separated the two sides of Witch Mountain. On the side with a road was Huautla, but on the other side of the mountain was the wild domain of *Chicón Nindo*, who was the Mazatecan *Quetzalcoatl*. From his cave of white quartz, *Chicón Nindo* had watched over the Little Ones' sanctuary since the first ritual of the Americas began. Now, standing in the mouth of that cave was Old Turtle who had long kept the ancient mythology alive and this Old Turtle was about to Ghost Dance.

THE OLD TURTLE

It was the moment after the animals of day went to sleep and before those of night awakened. The last living member of the Mazatec's original lineage of Ghost Dancers leaned on his staff and looked out over the cloud forest towards Huautla. At one hundred years of age, José Martínez was now called the Old Turtle because he was so old and moved so slowly. The Old Turtle was the hidden puppeteer, subtly pulling the strings behind the curtain on Witch Mountain and through this stage, the entire world.

A single beeswax candle illuminated the interior of a mountain shack with a tall, thatched roof. The Old Turtle's wife, the Old Turtle Woman, sat singing to *Chicón Nindo* like a *chachalaca* bird as she stirred a large *tesmole* pot of flying squirrel hanging over a fire. The Old Turtle kneeled before his altar and bathed himself in copal smoke. Then he spoke to his wife. "We perform the rituals of life so our generations can remember how to live. This is our dance."

Here where it first began, the original Ghost Dance survived untainted by the conquest. The Old Turtle washed himself with earth and then ever so slowly stood up, poised to dance with his head hung low. Continuing to stir the *tesmole*, the Old Turtle

Woman gently sang from her soul as the Old Turtle began to dance with tiny steps and delicate hand gestures.

Then the Old Turtle turned ever so slowly and looked across the canyon from Agua de Pozol towards Huautla. With nimble fingers he ritually tied together the streams of copal incense smoke, which represented the loose ends of the events he had just orchestrated in Huautla.

The Old Turtle took one pair of Little Ones but did not eat them. Instead, with his left hand he moved them across his body. At that moment a breeze blew, carrying the spores of the sacred Little Ones over the mountain gorge like vagabonds upon the wind. As the foreigners were forced onto a bus by the military, tiny invisible spores clung to their clothing. Three days later a rumor spread through the mountains that the Little Ones no longer spoke Mazatecan and now only communicated in English.

As the Old Turtle tied his last knot of smoke, the Old Turtle Woman stopped stirring the *tesmole*. The ritual used to manifest the Ghost Dance in modern times was now complete. Depleted of her strength by the ritual, the Old Turtle Woman reached out to her husband one last time and held him in her arms.

The Old Turtle hugged his wife gently as he laid her down on a straw mat and covered her with a blanket. She howled like an animal and then exhaled until the life faded from her body. The next day, the Old Turtle buried his wife under the Fertility Tree close to where she was born.

The Fertility Tree was a seedless virgin with long potent flowers that the women came to sit under when they wished to get pregnant. This tree was not native to the region. Julián Díaz-Ordaz brought its original seed when he built Rancho Catalunya in 1882. But ever since Ordaz's cook planted the first seed of the Fertility Tree and it grew, the Clean Sisters had coveted the very few seeds the tree produced annually for their fertility rite.

As the funeral ended, the Old Turtle, who had collected the Old Turtle Woman's last tears, mixed them with morning dew and sprinkled the teardrops on the tree. The sky rumbled and as night fell, the Earth Mother began to cry for her blessed Clean Sister. The Old Turtle had become a rainmaker and it rained for many days until the Mother took her Clean Sister back into the wet earth and the Old Turtle Woman was gone.

THE MAGIC MOMENT

The events that transpired in Huautla were just one more step in the ongoing ritual that the Old Turtle had begun when Julián Díaz-Ordaz arrived eighty-four years before. The original ritual was performed so people would rediscover the steps of the Ghost Dance in the hope of bringing back the Tree of Life and thereby maintain the human niche in the weave of nature. *Chicón Tokosho*, the Mazatec *Tezcatlipoca*, called the song, but *Chicón Nindo*, the Mazatec *Quetzalcoatl*, called the steps, as the modern world and the ancient past came together for a timeless dance on Witch Mountain.

Timothy Leary, the sacred clown and pied piper of mind expansion, had drawn the world's attention toward the mystery of plants even though he had turned to the modern gods of pharmaceuticals without the floral essence of the sacred mushroom being fully realized. Mushrooms had altered the mindset of an entire generation of young people and given them a glimpse beyond the Veil of Illusion. Timothy Leary's freestyle Ghost Dance had opened the door to possibility and pierced *Tezcatlipoca's* veil, but the Lord of Witches blocked the view before the youth of America could see what was behind the illusion.

CHAPTER 17
TURTLE MAGIC

The Old Turtle

T he Lord of Witches maintained his illusion in both the world of the living and that of the dead, preventing the skeletal traveler from seeing either his past or future. Like the youth of America, the Toltec Ghost Dancer sensed his purpose but could not find his direction. So the Ghost Dancer entered the next petal of the Black Flower and trudged through the Muck of

Self-Doubt towards the murky Swamp of Self-Loathing. Soon after, the Lord of Witches also arrived at the swamp's subterranean shore and found the Ghost Dancer sinking into this swamp.

MID-LEVEL OFFICERS

After the confrontation in Huautla, the psychedelic movement drifted away from the mountains of Oaxaca and the sacred mushrooms faded back into the mist. Huautla had become too dangerous a place for psychotropic fun and nearly all of the traumatized foreigners had left before they could cross over *Chato's* bridge into the true mystery.

During the 1970s, Mexico went through a rapid growth spurt and the ancient secrets kept moving deeper and deeper underground. The Modern Age of tourism and industrialization had hit Mexico like a fat *piñata*, and beaches, cities and ruins became the place to be, not hostile mountain hamlets. Without tourism and cattle ranching, the new Nescafé coffee plantations became the only way for the poor people of the region to make money.

Each year more and more cloud forests were cut down for the ever-expanding coffee plantations. Without the thick vegetation of the trees' canopy to hold the passing clouds, less rain fell and the moist ground became parched and dry. Environmental destruction was changing the climate of the Mountains of the Clouds and without sufficient water the locals began fighting over what little was left. Thirst escalated into a Witches War with witches killing each other over drinking water.

Here, where the cosmology of the Americas was born, the Old Turtle, the last of the original lineage of Ghost Dancers, sensed that the tipping point had arrived. But the Old Turtle knew that he could still speak with plants and might be able to convince *Tloloc Sequah* to bring more rain to end the worsening drought. The Old Turtle was part of the "old-time religion," and he performed the original uncorrupted version of the Ghost Dance taught to him directly by ancestral ghosts. He had waited for more than a hundred years to complete this ritual, a ritual that had begun before the outside world was aware of the hidden abilities of plants. The Old Turtle was now one hundred and twenty-seven years old and it was time for him to finish what he had started: tying his final knot in completion of the Ghost Dance of this calendar cycle.

The Old Turtle sat wrapped in a white sheet at the edge of the milky-white pool inside the Cave of the Fire God. Resting against the back wall was the skeleton of *Huehueteotl*'s first priest, surrounded by the earthly treasures he had been buried with: gold, beads and coral.

At dusk, a Clean Sister taught by the Old Turtle's wife lit a single beeswax candle and chanted in a low voice.

"Grandfather, I sit before you, a Daughter of the Moon and a Clean Sister. Hummingbirds of Dreams, come to claim the ghost of your beloved dancer."

The frogs sang as the Old Turtle began to slowly eat pairs of the variety of Little Ones they called the Children of the Dead. After consuming the Children of the Dead, the Old Turtle began to sing his death chant.

"Bones to dust and dust to soil, I will return to the Mother. Hummingbirds, I yearn to hear your hum. Grandfather Fire, I am ready to walk across the Milky Way. All my knots are tied but one. Now it is time to tie my final knot. Vision Serpent, open your mouth wide."

The Old Turtle then took thirteen jade beads and tossed them into the milky-white pool in the second chamber of the cave. In the ripples on the surface of the tiny pool the Old Turtle saw his vision and within the silence he could hear the hum of the approaching hummingbirds' rapidly beating wings. The hum increased as it was joined by the sounds of the buzzing insects and chirping frogs and this symphony of the forest began to warble, slowing down to what sounded like a marimba bubbling underwater.

A lone breeze blew into the cave and the Old Turtle turned to look. In a corner of the cave, barely seen in the flickering light, something stirred in the shadows. A soft voice spoke. "It is good to see you, old friend, but I, too, am dying."

The Old Turtle flinched with compassion and he whispered back, "Then it is time to dance with the ghosts."

Ever so slowly, the Old Turtle raised his ancient head and using his walking stick, lifted himself to his feet. Hunched over, as if this old Ghost Dancer was carrying the heavy burden of time upon his shoulders, he walked toward the cave entrance.

The Old Turtle stopped at the edge of the cliff high above what once was his beloved cloud forest below. Developers from outside the area had cut down most of the cloud forest to make pasture for cattle, turning floral abundance into a dry wasteland. Still, Venus, the Evening Star, had risen and twinkled bright blue in the sky. The Old Turtle opened his arms to the star, revealing his heart and crying out into the night.

"You witches who are driven by envy and greed and only dance for your own good without a care for the tribe of human beings, come feast upon the flesh of the old Ghost Dancer whom you've waited so long to consume!"

A breeze filled the night air with the scent of the dying Old Turtle and interrupted the momentary silence of the forest. Then, one by one, lifting their noses like hunting dogs, the *naguali* witches on the mountain sniffed the night air. With quivering nostrils they picked up the potent scent of the most sought-after kill of the calendar cycle: the last Ghost Dancer of the original lineage. Each witch's demonic *nagual* took flight, passing from dreams into the shadows of the night. Transforming from demons to bloodsucking insects, they flew low, stalking their precious prey to fulfill their lust for the kill.

With the rhythmic finesse of an orchestra leader the Old Turtle raised his bony left arm and the frogs sang. When he lowered his arm the frogs closed their mouths and went silent. The Old Turtle raised his arm again and, as if on cue, a donkey made a yodeling sound. When the Ghost Dancer dropped his arm a second time, the donkey immediately stopped and there was a long moment of silence.

José Martínez, the Old Turtle, struck his warrior stance with his staff raised as if he were a man a third his age. Lightning struck the staff, filling the Old Turtle with light as the Lord of the Mountain rumbled. Then, all at once, the remaining swarm of witches' *naguals* rushed the Old Turtle to feast upon his soul. Electrified by the lightning, the Old Turtle let out a primal scream that echoed through the canyons.

As the scream startled the night, out of the darkness came the most delicate fluttering of wings. The bat god Piquete-zina returned with an army of his kinsmen. In silence, the bats consumed the *naguals*, the insect totem spirits of marauding witches. Bracing himself upon his staff, the dying Old Turtle spoke.

"Master of the Dead, you know me. They call me the Worm Catcher."

Then the Old Turtle spat over and over on the ground until his spit formed a wet spot. Continuing his slow struggle to dance for all Americans, the Old Turtle took smaller and smaller steps. As he danced, the Old Turtle drew strands from his dripping spittle, pulling the saliva as far as it would stretch. Then he pantomimed tying a symbolic knot to the end of the staff. Using his staff as a bow, the Old Turtle tied a last remaining strand of spittle to an invisible arrow and ritually shot the arrow towards Venus, the Evening Star, like the dog-faced god had done in creating the four directions long ago.

When the lightning arrow pierced *Tezcatlipoca's* Veil of Illusion, it left a pulsating trail of light across the night sky. Moments later it hit its mark: Venus. Then, with a crack of thunder, what sounded like a chorus of angels rang through the night. The symbolic ritual that the Old Turtle had performed had arched off the distant star and someday would manifest at the end of the calendar cycle to destroy *Tezcatlipoca's* illusion. Step by step and inch by inch, the Old Turtle crawled back into the fire god's cave. Using his staff, he struggled with his last ounce of strength to make his final stand at the edge of the white pool. With his back to the cave entrance, the last words the Old Turtle whispered were very odd: "Mid-level officers, the final knot is yours to tie."

Then the Old Turtle fell facedown into the milky pool, crashing through its surface in a mass of exploding bubbles until his body floated in silence.

Moments later, the Clean Sister lifted the Old Turtle's white sheet off the surface of the pool's milky water and saw that the Old Turtle was gone and in his place a much younger Ghost Dancer emerged from the pool, gasping for a breath of life. When he caught his breath, the swaying Ghost Dancer howled like a beast. His mournful cry echoed through the Black Flower below and the Earth Mother sighed a sigh of relief after birthing her son back into life.

Few mourned the Old Turtle's death because he was part of a past that the now-evangelized Mazatecans would rather forget. So the Old Turtle's patron *Tloloc Sequah*, the rain god, grew angry at the people for not making the proper offering at the funeral of their rainmaker. In his anger, *Tloloc Sequah* cursed the people and, three days after his curse, an evangelized Mazatecan woman was found dead in a nearby creek. The old people believed that when a woman died in a creek the rains would not come, but the young people tried to ignore this omen and pass it off as superstition.

In the church of Chilchotla many people prayed for rain but to no avail. It was the rainy season, but the clouds passed by without leaving a drop of water behind. Three months after the Old Turtle's death, thick clouds rolled in from Veracruz and it began to drizzle. The locals were exuberant, but what began as soft drops of rain quickly escalated into hailstones the size of oranges.

The Mazatecans had never seen ice fall from the sky and they huddled together in their thatched huts waiting for the freak storm to pass. When the hail ended and they ventured outside to assess the damage, the locals found their crops destroyed and their livestock dead. In the forest, many of the birds and small animals had also been killed, and the Little Ones had disappeared.

After thousands of years, the Fruit of the original Ghost Dance had gone extinct, seemingly overnight. Even though the tropical hailstorm only lasted a moment, the repercussions of its fallout would change the people's lives forever and would eventually alter the course of American history.

The frightened Mazatecans struggled amongst themselves to come to terms with the catastrophe. Some said the witch José Martínez had cursed them on his deathbed because they had forgotten their traditional ways and they had angered the rain god, *Tloloc Sequah,* and *Chicón Nindo*, the Lord of the Mountain.

CHAPTER 18
IMPOSTOR CORN

Lady Xoc Ghost Dancing

Like the Mazatec, the Toltec Ghost Dancer was also immersed in a swamp of hopelessness. The six ordeals had taken their toll and now the exhausted Toltec sank slowly into an endless quicksand. Because fighting only made him sink faster, the Ghost Dancer resigned himself to the futility of the situation and put his life in the hands of the gods.

But just before his head disappeared under the murky surface, he saw a black bee hovering in the air above him, buzzing and circling, until finally the bee landed and stung the Toltec. The sting sent the Ghost Dancer into a frenzy that should have engulfed him, but his flailing hand managed to latch onto a submerged branch of a tree and he pulled himself out of the depths, covered in grime and gasping for air. Hidden by the fog sent to blind him, the Toltec escaped, dragging his tired bones towards the next petal of the Black Flower: the realm of *Centeotl*, the corn god. This was the petal where the ants stored sacred corn and where bees were born to spread pollen, for corn cannot exist without ants and bees.

Believing that the pesky Toltec had drowned in the muck of his own self-loathing, the Lord of Witches was now ready to turn his attention to his next great illusion: impostor corn. *Tezcatlipoca* visualized the corn in his smoky Black Mirror. Though the corn looked perfect on the outside, the inside was as hollow as a discarded husk. Resistant to insects, easy to plant and with the ability to produce larger harvests, this corn would seem to be an ideal crop. But it would have no substance and, rather than providing nourishment, it would harm the bees and weaken the people, making them easy prey for the Plague Mother's white worms of disease. Now, all the Lord of Witches needed was a way to introduce his poison corn to the people.

When the haze of his Black Mirror cleared, *Tezcatlipoca* realized that the Mazatecan disaster was the opportunity he had been looking for. So the Lord of Witches huffed and puffed and blew a magical smoke through the mirror and into the boardroom where Mexican commodities were being brokered. As the unseen smoke of illusion clouded the room, a plan formed in the minds of those in charge: Monsanto's genetically altered corn would be introduced into the Sierra Mazateca to relieve the famine that had resulted from the hailstorm.

CORN MAGIC

Although the Mexican government had promised the Mazatecans the corn was on the way, its arrival was constantly delayed. So by the time the bioengineered miracle corn finally made its way up into the mountains, the Mazatecans had starved for four months, and in the meantime, they had replanted and harvested their own corn crops. In one hand, they held the corn that the lord *Quetzalcoatl* had built civilization upon and in the other, *Tezcatlipoca's* pale imposter corn. The choice was clear and the Mazatecans proudly refused the long-overdue government handout.

The Old Turtle's final Ghost Dance had manifested a hailstorm of change that led to the Mazatecan's rejection of *Tezcatlipoca's* impostor corn. This rejection set into motion a series of events that would change the course of American history, igniting a revolution in the land of the Mayan kings that would eventually spread across all of Latin America.

Not one to fight a losing battle and unwilling to waste any more time, *Tezcatlipoca* left the Mazateca and turned his attention south towards Chiapas, the ancestral home of the Maya. Because the Mayans had much more land than the Mazatecans, they were known to be far less ornery. Mexico's poorest and most isolated farming state appeared to be fertile ground for the imposter corn, but things are not always what they seem. The only thing that was certain was that *Tezcatlipoca* was about to lead the Mexican government out of a Mazatecan frying pan and into a Mayan fire.

On January 1, 1994, a masked group of Mayan Indians danced to raise the ghosts of Zapata's revolution from the grave before the group stormed the Hall of Records in the mountain pueblo of San Cristóbal de las Casas. Calling themselves *Zapatistas* in honor of the famed Indian revolutionary, these Mayan women and men burned the land deeds to their own *ejidos*, or community property. Without these deeds, the *ejidos* could not be transferred to generals in the Mexican army who wanted to force the sale of the *indios'* communal land to grow *Tezcatlipoca's* imposter corn. Under the guise of the newly implemented North American Free Trade Agreement, or NAFTA, the Lord of Witches had created one of his greatest illusions.

Ejidos were plots of land planted by each village for any tribal member whose crop had failed. During the conquest, the Spanish Crown had outlawed this pre-Columbian practice, but it was reinstated in the 16th century by Padre Bartolomé de las Casas.

Many of the Mayan Indians who stormed the sleepy mountain hamlet of San Cristóbal were still in tribal dress and carrying sticks made to look like rifles. They weren't soldiers, but rather farmers, afraid of losing the little they still had. The generals in charge wanted to send in troops, but the Mexican government feared an international public relations scandal and decided on an old technique that had worked in the past.

The month after the burning of the deeds in San Cristóbal, the largest witches war since the conquest erupted in Chiapas. Witches from outside of Chiapas had been hired by the military to kill and terrorize tribes supporting the *Zapatistas*. The witches' weapon of choice was magic instead of guns. But the Zinacantán, Chamula, Huixtán, Ch'ol, Oxhuc, and Tenejapa tribes fought back, using their own witches to drive out *Tezcatlipoca's* foot soldiers.

While the Mayans were busy waging their Witches War, the government used mercenaries to eliminate anyone who resisted the planting of *Tezcatlipoca's* impostor corn. When harvest time came it was the bioengineered corn not witchcraft or the paramilitary units that almost broke the rebellion. Cheaper to produce, the GMO corn outsold the more labor intensive, traditional corn and collapsed the market. This left the Mayans with nothing to sell except what the generals wanted in the first place: the *ejidos*. So the *Zapatistas* did what any retreating Indians would do in their tenuous situation: they ran and hid, in the Lacandon Jungle.

LADY XOC

The *Zapatistas* found temporary sanctuary in the last enclaves of old-growth trees which shrouded the ancient Mayan ruins of Yaxchilán. Here, where the remote Lacandon Mayans still came to ghost dance with the old gods, the jungle was alive with the sound of squawking parrots and roaring howler monkeys.

Without roads, the military was reluctant to continue its pursuit of the rebels into the dense rain forest and this gave the tattered *Zapatistas* time to regroup. But unbeknownst to the Mayan rebels, they were about to make their last stand at the tomb of a Ghost Dancer unlike all the rest.

Lady Xoc, the charismatic 8th-century Mayan Queen of Yaxchilán, was as famous as any modern-day celebrity. Beloved by her constituents, Lady Xoc was one of the very few women who ghost danced without being a member of the Clean Sisterhood. During her lifetime, Lady Xoc broke all the rules, bringing the Ghost Dance out of the hidden world of ancient mysticism and transforming the ritual into a public extravaganza. She used the ceremonial center of Yaxchilán to promote herself as a ghost-dancing prophet of the royal bloodline and became the most popular queen of Mayan history. In honor of her accomplishments, Lady Xoc's tomb was built next to the tombs of the kings in the acropolis of Yaxchilán.

Seeking sanctuary, over a thousand years later, the *Zapatistas* entered the ruins and stumbled upon this ancient tomb. They had no way of knowing that Lady Xoc's ability to use the media to unite her people through the Ghost Dance would turn out to be crucial to their future survival.

Lady Xoc's passing enshrined her ancestral glory for eternity since she had her scribes engrave her tomb with detailed lintels depicting her in all different stages of a classic Ghost Dance ritual. Each lintel was placed above the entryways of the descending sections of her crypt, leading in succession to the burial chamber where she was ultimately laid to rest.

These lintels told the story of Lady Xoc's transformation while using sacramental plants to commune with the ghost of her most important ancestor, the founder of Yaxchilán: Jaguar Penis Knot.

In the lintel depictions, Lady Xoc watches the swirls of rising incense smoke form a two-headed Vision Serpent. Then, Jaguar Penis Knot's ghostly body emerges from the open mouth of the serpent with a fire lance in his hand, the Mayan symbol for the Tree of Life. Lady Xoc used the lintel inscriptions of her Ghost Dance with Jaguar Penis Knot to reaffirm in stone her direct bloodline to her grandfather. This helped establish Lady Xoc, rather than her husband King Jaguar Shield, as the direct heir to the throne and her popularity soared like a Plumed Serpent.

By promoting the arts, healing and music, Lady Xoc helped to lift the Mayan world to one of its highest peaks of civilization. Her success attracted many followers and Yaxchilán grew until it became an overpopulated metropolis. But the resources needed to maintain her city ultimately began to diminish as Lady Xoc became obsessed with her own legacy. Too busy to venture into the forests beyond the city, the Mayan queen lost her connection with the tribes and the gods of nature.

Seeing herself as greater than the gods and spirits of nature, Lady Xoc gave orders to cut down entire forests just to make the plaster whitewash that was used to cover the temples so they could be painted in glorious colors. To feed the overpopulated city, all the animals of the forest were hunted and the rivers turned filthy with the sewage waste of urban sprawl. With the trees gone, a drought began and Lady Xoc prayed for rain, but the old gods of nature were angry that the people had disgraced their creation and no longer blessed the Mayans lands with good weather.

The Mayans were about to learn the hard way the same simple truth that their ancestors had lived by: without a seasonal pattern of sun and rain, civilization could not be sustained. So the wealthy city people left Yaxchilán and migrated to the forest in search of food and water. Arriving there, they found the relatives of the people they had sacrificed to their gods and enslaved to build their temples. These hungry forest people consumed and turned to ash the bones of the fattened city dwellers who had mercilessly sacrificed their children to appease angry gods.

During one of the worst droughts in Mayan history, Lady Xoc, the Queen of Yaxchilán, died and her spirit was depicted following a swarm of glistening butterflies over the Milky Way and down the throat of the Celestial Vision Serpent. Then the ghost of Lady Xoc came to rest in a petal of the Black Flower where she slept for a thousand years until a gallant young freedom fighter appeared in the haze of her endless dream.

Armed with a shotgun, dual bandoleers across his chest, and the eyes of a poet, Subcomandante Marcos stepped out of the jungle mist. The *Zapatista* took off his ski mask and lit his trademark pipe as he wandered through the ruins of Yaxchilán's acropolis. Marcos and his fellow *Zapatistas* were trapped by military troops in Lady Xoc's ancient home. Cut off and surrounded, the *Zapatistas* had no means to communicate their plight to the outside world and were unable to defend themselves in the media. The Mexican news had portrayed the *Zapatistas* as nothing more than radical insurgents led by an outside communist agitator.

Drawn to the protection of Lady Xoc's tomb, Subcomandante Marcos stood in front of the acropolis where she had once ghost danced to win the favor of the gods. He could almost feel the ancient spirits of the ruined city come alive as he lit his pipe, sending billows of smoke up into the humid jungle air. The pipe smoke rose above Marcos' head, twisting and turning until it took the form of a Vision Serpent.

The ghost of Lady Xoc awoke as the Vision Serpent opened its smoky mouth and Lady Xoc's vaporous body entered the world of the living. The Mayan queen had slept for an eternity in a paradise petal of the Black Flower and was now joyful to have the opportunity to dance with this handsome young man whom she was about to bless with her power of celebrity. Unseen by Marcos, Lady Xoc's ghostly image danced through the shadows of the ruins, whispering ancient words of wisdom into his ear as if they were his own thoughts.

Her words would guide him through the veils of *Tezcatlipoca's* illusion towards a solution that would bring the obscure *Zapatistas* to the forefront of the world's stage.

From behind the folds of Lady Xoc's skirt, the *Zapatistas* launched the first internet revolution in history. The *Zapatistas* had devised a way to get around *Tezcatlipoca's* illusion so that their side of the story could be known. To tell this story, the internet, a pinnacle of modernity, was used by computer-savvy compatriots of the *Zapatistas* to post charismatic images of the man Lady Xoc had whispered to. Smoking a pipe through a black ski mask, Subcomandante Marcos, a classic Latin American poet revolutionary, won the hearts of women with the gift of celebrity he received from Lady Xoc.

Because powerful female celebrities romanticized the young Marcos, who was an articulate and passionate speaker, he was able to begin a conversation with the outside world about human rights. Via the World Wide Web he explained the *Zapatistas'* struggle against tyranny and how NAFTA and its GMO corn would bring about the end of the Mayan people. Then Marcos took the campaign a step further as he spoke about the importance of indigenous people in the struggle to defend the Mother Earth against exploiters. Marcos understood that while he was fighting for ideals, the Zapatistas were fighting for their lives.

Fearing retribution against his family, Marcos kept his identity hidden behind a mask as he won the hearts of peasants, common people and celebrities alike. His insight into the importance of indigenous people in the struggle to stop environmental destruction opened the eyes of many sympathizers around the world. The *Zapatistas* weren't only struggling to hold on to their land and culture, they were also fighting to stop the pollution of the planet with bioengineered crops, chemical fertilizers, herbicides and pesticides.

Celebrities and other powerful *Zapatista* sympathizers around the world used the Internet to pressure the Mexican government into calling a truce. While the authorities reluctantly agreed to the terms of the temporary ceasefire, they did not pull back their troops. But the *Zapatistas* used this ceasefire to build hospitals and schools in villages that had never had them before, and in honor of their beloved compatriot Subcomandante Marcos, the first letter of the names of the villages they chose spelled out his name. The villages were Margarita, Acteal, Reforma, Comitán, Ocosingo and Soledad: MARCOS.

On Christmas Eve, 1997, while the ceasefire was still in effect, a mercenary unit arrived in the *Zapatista*-controlled mountain village of Acteal. Entering the church during mass, the mercenaries did not find armed rebels. Instead, they came upon mothers and their children and the elderly, but they nonetheless savagely murdered forty-five unarmed members of the *Zapatistas'* families and mutilated their bodies.

After this Christmas massacre, international civil rights activists demanded that the government maintain the promised truce by protecting the Mayans against the paramilitary death squads. The Mexican government responded by denying they had hired the mercenaries and then warned the *Zapatistas* that the only way they could protect themselves from further attacks would be by turning themselves in.

In spite of their losses, the *Zapatistas* continued to resist and reached out to President Bill Clinton through celebrity supporters. The Mayans asked Clinton to intercede and stop further massacres. Fearful that a mounting revolution south of the border could hurt his brainchild, NAFTA, Clinton turned a deaf ear to the Mayan cause and gave his support to the military instead of the freedom fighters.

After the New Year, US-made tanks rolled into the main plazas of the shantytowns surrounding the Lacandon Jungle. The tanks were supported by over 35,000 Mexican troops in a land, river and air assault designed to decimate the now-demoralized and heartbroken *Zapatistas*. When the orders were given, the columns of soldiers and tanks slowly advanced from Ocosingo towards the lost city of Yaxchilán.

Out in the jungle, the possibility of an ambush buzzed around the military convoy like a swarm of mosquitoes. When the unarmed *Zapatistas* appeared from the dense foliage waving a white flag, Colonel Cuevas and the other mid-level officers ordered the skittish troops not to fire.

Wearing their traditional tribal clothing, the *Zapatistas* smiled at the soldiers and greeted them in colloquial Spanish. "This is not a military zone. This is an indigenous zone. Look at us," they said. "We're *indios* just like you. Why would you hurt us for doing what your own families would do to feed their starving children? We're not the enemy, we're you!"

Hit by words more powerful than bullets, Colonel Cuevas and his soldiers turned and looked at each other. The *Zapatistas* were right. Like many of his soldiers, Cuevas was a pure-blood Indian, a Mazatecan from Huautla, and he realized that the *Zapatistas* looked more like his relatives than his enemies.

Colonel Cuevas had been a soldier for many years and was trained to follow orders, but his spit-polished veneer had begun to crack. He had seen the aftermath of the massacre at Acteal and it had sickened him. The last thing Cuevas wanted was another massacre, so he called a field officers' meeting and together the officers decided to halt the siege.

When the *Zapatistas* realized the soldiers had become sympathetic to their cause, they became so excited they began to laugh and cry at the same time. Emotionally overwhelmed themselves, the soldiers couldn't help but join in. Just as the Old Turtle had predicted, the noncommissioned officers of indigenous descent had picked up the steps to the Ghost Dance.

Within hours, webcast images of the *Zapatistas* laughing and crying along with Mexican soldiers were broadcast internationally. Because the entire world had watched as the officers refused to kill the *Zapatistas*, the Mexican government was forced into making a peace treaty with the rebels. Although the treaty allowed the *Zapatistas* to continue their outreach programs building hospitals and schools, it did not stop NAFTA, nor did it stop the impostor corn. However, the nail of NAFTA, which was to be the last in the Mexican Indians' coffin, instead hit Mayan jade, ringing out a cry of resistance throughout the Americas.

CHAPTER 19
KON TIKI VIRACOCHA

Kon Tiki Viracocha

B efore the Toltec Ghost Dancer could reach the next petal of the Black Flower he would have to cross a deep crevice. The Toltec people knew of this place and called it the Hall of Records, or the Great Book. Within this crystalline cave of endless honeycombs lay all the knowledge the ancestors had gathered together from time immemorial. This hive of ancient secrets was also where the Clean Sisters had concealed the steps of the Ghost Dance.

Knowing that he needed these hidden secrets to continue his journey to mend the Rope of the Dead, the Ghost Dancer let go of his fear and willingly fell into the bottomless pit of knowledge. The billowy honeycombs formed from the wisdom of the ages broke his fall and he curled up in a fetal position among them to rest. As the Toltec slept, the echoes of history reverberated off the crystalline walls of the Hall of Records and entered his dreams, speaking to him in the voice of the ancestors. The ancestors told him that the only way he could learn the missing steps of the Ghost Dance was by learning the wisdom of all four directions: east, south, west and north. For even though the Toltec Ghost Dancer had followed the dance across North America and Mexico, to the north, east and west, he had yet to follow it south.

As the Toltec stretched out his arm, moving it in the direction of the south, a page of the Great Book turned also, following his motion. On this next page the Toltec saw an ancient Peruvian city called Caral. As the images of Caral came into focus, the Ghost Dancer noticed intricately irrigated green corn and endless white cotton fields surrounding a central plaza. Under sunny, blue skies, the inhabitants collected the cotton and wove it into finely made fishnets on backstrap looms. This scene illustrates the birth of irrigation and the growth of domestic cotton in the Americas which occurred at the same time that corn was domesticated in Mexico.

The next image that unfolded in the Great Book was of fishermen arriving from the coast carrying baskets full of fish and other seafood. The fisherman had great respect for the high-quality craftsmanship of the people of Caral and happily traded their seafood for nets made by the city's weavers. The people of

Caral also valued the fishermen for providing them with food that did not deplete their local forest and so the people traded their nets to the fishermen for a fair value.

The Toltec Ghost Dancer began to wonder why envy and greed had not weakened the people of Caral in the same way it had his descendants in Mexico. The Great Book showed him that at the same time Caral flourished, Mexico also had enjoyed a golden era of a thousand years of peace under the rule of *Quetzalcoatl* and Precious Flower, but it had fallen from grace when *Tezcatlipoca* cut the Rope of the Dead.

Unfolding the pages of the Great Book, the Toltec Ghost Dancer observed that the people of Caral, like his Mexican ancestors, had an esoteric order of Clean Sisters and Ghost Dancers. They also believed that the Rope of the Dead was the umbilical cord that connected their city to the Tree of Life. The only difference was that the Ghost Dancers of Caral did not have the Little Ones as their sacrament, but instead used a brew called *ayahuasca* made from a talking vine. Through the vision inspired by this vine, the Ghost Dancers procured the aid of their ancestors who in turn could petition the gods of the elements to bless them with the gift of good weather. Thus the rain and wind were in sync with the seasons and so the crops were plentiful.

As the Toltec Ghost Dancer continued to focus on the details of the Great Book, he saw that there were no military installations in Caral, nor signs of battles nor of wars. The people did not have to fight with their neighbors to survive. Instead, they were honored for the quality of their achievements.

Caral's patron god, *Kon Tiki Viracocha*, who watched over the city, was the South American equivalent of *Quetzalcoatl*. The human manifestation of *Kon Tiki* was also a bearded stranger who had come from the sea and later became a god when his spirit took flight through the Ghost Dance. Like his Mexican counterpart, he became known as the god of civilization. And *Kon Tiki* had arrived in South America at approximately the same time *Quetzalcoatl* washed ashore on the Mexican coast.

When the Lord of Witches severed the Rope of the Dead, both civilizations, Mexican and Peruvian, lost the means to communicate with the spirits in nature and so the weather turned.

Droughts, floods and plagues of insects sucked the life force from the land, and without good weather, the people of Caral lost both faith in the gods and their respect for Mother Nature.

Turning their backs on the heart of what had empowered them, the people of Caral soon saw their forests destroyed for frivolous reasons. This destruction of the environment caused climatic change that finally destroyed the city of eternal peace. All that remained was the myth that one day the bearded *Kon Tiki* would return from the east and bring back the golden era of peace and harmony.

THE VISION SERPENT

A Quechua soothsayer in the Andes Mountains of Peru cut open a guinea pig and read its entrails. Fever had ravaged the small rodent's organs so they appeared rotten and smelled awful. The soothsayer cried, for this was a terrible omen that a deadly vapor of disease called the *xawara* would soon cover the land. The soothsayer foresaw that new epidemics like the ones Columbus had first brought to the New World would again arrive with a foreign invader from across the seas.

Dark storm clouds and bloody trails followed the brutal Pizarro brothers' expedition across the Andes Mountains of South America. In 1532, thousands of years after the Golden Age of Caral had faded to dust, these gold-hungry conquistadors searched for El Dorado, the legendary place where the Inca once mined their gold. With rotting boils under their armor and heads full of lice, the conquistadors were plagued by fevered dreams. Their thoughts swung between golden delusions of grandeur and fear of becoming human sacrifices to appease the angry Incas' gods.

It had been forty years since Columbus returned to Spain from his maiden voyage to the Americas with stories of a kingdom of gold deep in the jungle: El Dorado. Before the Pizarro brothers arrived in South America, Hernán Cortés had discovered the golden capital of the Aztec and believed he had found El Dorado. However, fourteen years later, on an expedition led by his brother General Francisco Pizarro, Captain Hernando Pizarro heard the same legend of a land of gold in the Andes Mountains of Ecuador. The informant told the captain there was a tribe in the jungle, the "Yanomami" who were so rich in the sunstone that every day their ruler, or *cacique*, covered himself in gold dust before bathing in a lake named Parima. They called him and the source of his gold the Golden One, or El Dorado.

Blind faith and draconian rule kept the sick soldiers walking through the valleys of death and back up into the frozen wind-swept mountains, where the scavenging condor ruled. Fearing for their souls even more than their lives, the conquistadors' *padres* convinced these simple soldiers that the tropical fevers they were suffering from were demonic tortures brought on by local witches to test their Christian faith.

The *conquistadores* had no way of knowing that they were actually the ones that brought these diseases, such as dengue fever, yellow fever and malaria. Once introduced by the Europeans, mosquitoes spread the diseases. There were no pandemics of infectious diseases in the Americas before the Europeans arrived, and because of this, the indigenous people had no resistance to the ravaging plagues that descended upon them.

General Francisco Pizarro's disease-infested conquistadors entered the Incas' empire and were awestruck by the golden grandeur. Yet at the same time they were deeply disturbed by the pagan spectacle of the Incas' version of the Ghost Dance. In sacrament-induced rapture, the Indians paraded the mummies of their kings and dead relatives around on gilded litters, dancing and singing happily under the influence of *coca* tea, *virola* snuff and *chicha* beer.

The bodies of the dead had been mummified with *coca* leaves and gray tobacco and were dressed in fine textiles, brightly colored feathers and precious metals. This was the Incas' version of the Ghost Dance of *Kon Tiki Viracocha*, a ceremony called the *Aya Marcay Quilla*, or "Full Body Coming out of the Mouth." A shared belief of many of the Pan-American tribes was that the full body of the ancestral ghosts manifested in the world of the living through the mouth of the Vision Serpent.

General Francisco Pizarro attempted to stop the *Aya Marcay Quilla* Ghost Dance with lances and swords but failed, though the vapors of the *xawara* did not. As the Quechua continued to ghost dance with the mummified bodies of their dead relatives, their living relatives began to die all around them. When the smallpox hit, the Pizarro brothers retreated from the city and then encircled it, so no one could leave.

By the time the *Aya Marcay Quilla* ceremony ended, most of the residents inside the Incas' capital city had died or were too sick to defend themselves. Then General Pizarro's troops rushed in and captured the Inca prince Atahualpa, forcing him to pay a huge ransom for his life. Atahualpa petitioned the wealthiest of his kingdom to bring all their golden objects to him to pay the ransom.

General Pizarro promised Atahualpa, "As God is my witness, I will leave with my troops once the ransom is paid."

After the mega-fortune in golden ransom arrived, General Pizarro noticed that all the gold the Inca prince brought him was already refined and worked. So General Pizarro broke his word and tortured the young Atahualpa to find out the location of the gold mines of El Dorado. Only after his feet were burned to charred stumps did the proud Atahualpa tell General Pizarro. "The sun stones of my kingdom come from a lake called Parima. Parima is in the jungle below the original Tree of Life that divides the two great rivers." Then Atahualpa, the Inca Prince, raised his head and cursed General Pizarro.

"The ancestors have told me that you conquistadors will never find El Dorado, but in future generations your descendants will. When they do, our god of coca will bring misery to your children's children in return for the treachery you have brought us. Then, the *Pacha Mama*, the Earth Mother, will remove the blight of your children from the land with a great flood."

This was the first time the Prophecy of Seven Generations was used for vengeance. After making his curse, Atahualpa was strangled to death by the conquistadors, and shortly after Atahualpa's death, Pizarro also assassinated the last Inca king, Tupac. Before Tupac was drawn and quartered, he told the conquistador leader, "I am one, but the pieces of my body will become many and they will take back our land." Aguirre, Pizarro's deranged captain, as well as the explorer Sir Francis Drake, searched the Orinoco River for El Dorado but never found Lake Parima.

After the *Aya Marcay Quilla* Ghost Dance ceremony was outlawed, the colonial era began and the tribes that were able to escape gradually retreated into the protection of the Amazon Jungle. During the colonial era, expeditions to find gold in

Amazonia were met by both the resistance of these tribes and a hostile environment filled with swarms of biting insects, mud, poisonous plants and deadly animals. The dangers of the Amazon Jungle allowed well-concealed tribes to hide behind Mother Nature's ferocity and maintain their culture, while contacted tribesmen who survived the illnesses were slaughtered, baptized or enslaved.

THE VINE OF THE DEAD

For centuries after the conquest, the Amazon Jungle remained a powerful and impenetrable adversary. The European methods of warfare, including the use of horses, heavy armor and cannons, proved unsuitable for the Amazonian terrain and the jungle was able to keep her treasures well hidden. While the rest of the world moved on and empires rose and fell, the tribes of the jungle danced to a different drum, maintaining their culture without ever having contact with the outside world. But four centuries of near-complete isolation ended in the early twentieth century when armed men swarmed into the jungle searching for rubber trees.

Necessity is the mother of invention and the newly emerging automobile industry needed rubber to make tires. Rubber trees only grew in the Amazon Jungle, so enormous amounts of money and equipment were shipped to the jungle to begin the harvest and export of these newly precious trees. Overnight, rubber became like black gold and great fortunes were made harvesting this coveted tree sap. With more and more rubber cutters entering the jungle, the number of violent conflicts with local tribes also grew.

But the Amahuaca of Peru resisted the invasion of the rubber cutters better than most. One of their chiefs in particular, Xumu, was an accomplished Ghost Dancer and he led their resistance. Xumu was so in tune with the ghosts and the environment around him that he could perceive the outcome of events that were yet to take place. Xumu had a vision that the ancestors were going to send him a young foreigner to help drive out the violent and diseased rubber cutters who were polluting the Amahuaca homeland.

In 1924, while working as a camp boy for a group of Peruvian rubber cutters, Manuel Córdova Díaz was kidnapped by Xumu's tribe: the Honi Kui. For months Díaz went through an austere cleansing process in which he took herbal baths and purges to gain back his health and thrive in the jungle environment.

Then the old chief had tribal members teach the boy the skills needed to survive in his new environment, and after a time, Díaz was adopted into the tribe. What Díaz did not know was that the baths and purges the old chief had put him through not only made him stronger, they also cleansed his soul and prepared him for learning the Ghost Dance.

Díaz and Xumu sat silently together in the middle of a clearing while an elderly couple prepared the *ayahuasca* brew in an ancient urn. The yellow vine had been cold pressed in the urn along with another plant, the leaves of which were the same color as the markings of a boa constrictor. The ceremony began at dusk, as the chief began to chant during the moment of silence when the animals of the day go to the sleep and the creatures of night awaken.

Díaz drank from the urn and then vomited up the last of the poison of the outside world that remained in him. As Díaz entered into the world of the ghosts, images of the *hekura*, all the spirits of the jungle's animals, flew, ran and crawled through his mind. Xumu chanted until his own spirit animal flew into Díaz's vision and led him past the chaos to a tree where the boy then saw his own spirit guide for the first time.

All talking plants have their own song, and the Vine of the Dead's song was a rhythmic rustling of dry leaves that blended in harmony with the sound of a rattlesnake *maraca*.

Díaz's own spirit animal then took over and led him directly to the Spirit of the Vine, which appeared from the darkness as a black panther. The large cat led Díaz into the Black Flower where he saw the ghost of the Toltec Ghost Dancer resting on illuminated honeycombs.

Here in the Black Flower, the Ghost Dancer opened the Great Book to Díaz and for the first time Díaz peered into the world of the dead and began to learn the knowledge of the ancestral ghosts.

There was no apprentice program in Pan-American mysticism. Instead Xumu's ancestors had learned directly from the plants and spirits. Using *ayahuasca* to tap into the forest's brain network, these ancestors gained access to plant knowledge which was then interpreted and applied for medical and other uses. These same ancestral ghosts who had taught Xumu were now teaching Díaz about "the nature of things" and "the order of life," wisdom which the stars above, the living and the dead, the animals and the plants all lived by.

Díaz was led to a tree in the forest that was filled with red howler monkeys. But instead of hunting the monkeys with their blowguns, the Honi Kui waited with old Xumu in silence. The monkeys chanted in tandem until an elderly white howler monkey appeared on a high branch of a huge tree that stood next to the other howlers. On cue, the monkeys fell silent and when the old white monkey raised his palms to the sun and let out a single hoot, the others all answered in a chorus of howls. Each time the old monkey dropped and raised his palms back up to the sun, the other monkeys stopped and howled again, raising their own palms in an orchestrated response.

Manuel Córdova Díaz had witnessed a hidden secret of the jungle: the spiritual communion of non-human animals. This experience opened his mind to possibilities of awareness beyond the accepted norm of the time and changed his entire view of Xumu's teachings, for Díaz realized that, except for a handful of old medicine people who lived in the most remote place on earth, these ancient beliefs had mostly disappeared. Díaz now understood that the old chief had given him an opportunity to enter a different reality.

As Díaz began to explore his new awareness, international companies seeking wood invaded the jungle. The forests, including the monkeys' trees, were cut down and the howler monkeys stopped praying. During this time Xumu died and there was one fewer medicine person who still knew the path to the hidden world of plants and ghosts. But fortunately for the outside world, Manuel Córdova Díaz had learned the skills taught to him by Xumu.

After Xumu's death, Díaz left the Honi Kui and returned to the "civilized" world, making his home in the Amazon port town of Iquitos, Peru. As the great healers such as Xumu faded from history, Díaz became a living artifact who had learned a lost knowledge firsthand. He would also ultimately be the one who would bring the ancestral knowledge of the Amazon to the outside world.

As a grown man in Iquitos, Manuel Córdova Díaz collected and recorded more curative jungle plants than anyone ever had before. During his long lifetime, Díaz continued to cure peasants and Indians along with presidents, generals and many international dignitaries. He never hid the fact that he diagnosed patients by taking *ayahuasca* and consulting with the ancestral ghost of his mentor, Xumu.

Plants that Díaz collected were shipped to botanical gardens and museums around the world and stories of his amazing abilities spread as far as New York and Europe. Díaz had become one of South America's most renowned healers, a Ghost Dancer and a man who had made the modern world aware of the healing botanical treasures of the Amazon.

The rubber boom ended when the seeds of rubber trees were smuggled into Asia and were grown less expensively on giant plantations. By then, through Manuel Córdoba Díaz and others who followed in his footsteps, the outside world was becoming increasingly aware of the seemingly endless natural resources of Amazonia.

But Díaz's knowledge became a double-edged machete as the events of his life began to attract others who came only to exploit the Amazon's resources. Every day, more and more intruders began to encroach on the Indian land in search of hardwood, minerals and plants, and the Amazon Jungle became ripe for the picking. Among the treasure hunters, there soon arrived a new and different type of intruder. This invader was not interested in the jungle's natural resources. Instead, it had come to harvest souls.

SECTION 3
THE PRESENT

CHAPTER 20
THE SAINTS OF THE AMAZON

Cerro Pintado

The Toltec Ghost Dancer crawled out of the Hall of Records with renewed hope and continued to follow the Rope of the Dead toward the Tree of Life. The rope led him through a petrified forest to a dark petal where the Lord of Days stood in front of his obsidian Black Mirror. The Toltec hid behind the curved edge of the petal, but the Lord of Witches caught a glimpse of his reflection in the smoky mirror. Believing he was hidden from view, the Ghost Dancer watched *Tezcatlipoca's* ritual that, seeing an opportunity for trickery, the god now performed for the Ghost Dancer.

The Lord of Witches did a magical sleight of hand, creating an illusion that he hoped would lead to the eventual destruction of humanity. From the smoky mirror *Tezcatlipoca* pulled a carved jaguar bone dripping in black blood. It looked like the *tiponi*, the sacred object that gave authority over the land, and now the Lord of Witches appeared to have it in his grasp.

Watching this illusion unfold in front of him led the Ghost Dancer to believe that the Lord of Witches had collected the seven hidden pieces of the *tiponi* and made them whole again. As the Ghost Dancer watched, *Tezcatlipoca* completed his ritual and retired to bed, seemingly secure in his control of the sacred object.

While *Tezcatlipoca* faked sleep, the Toltec Ghost Dancer stealthily snuck up to the altar and stole back what he thought was the *tiponi*. Then the Ghost Dancer ran for his life, heading back towards the ancestral ghosts of the tribe where he had hidden one of the seven pieces of the sacred jaguar bone. When the Toltec arrived at the village of the Kogi's ancestors, he finally stopped running, but when he opened his hand he found it empty. The Lord of Witches had tricked him in order to find out where the Toltec had hidden a piece of the *tiponi*.

The Toltec had accidently led *Tezcatlipoca* to one of the seven tribes where he had hidden a shard. From here, *Tezcatlipoca* could follow the trail to the other six pieces and take back authority over the land.

OIL AND SOULS

After World War I, automobiles replaced horses as the most common mode of transportation and mass production soon created a need for oil to keep these cars on the road. By the time

World War II ended almost thirty years later, oil had become the life blood whose circulation kept the body of the modern world moving. Feeling destined to supply the growing global demand, Nelson Rockefeller, the grandson of the oil baron John D. Rockefeller, sent crews to explore for oil in the remote Amazon Jungle, the immune system of the Americas. Blinded by *Tezcatlipoca's* illusion, Rockefeller had no idea that he was a participant in the completion of a ritual that had begun thousands of years before.

Though it was believed that the last uncontacted tribes on earth had been discovered in New Guinea during World War II, when the oil exploration crews arrived in the Amazon Jungle, they found naked tribesman hiding behind every tree. The heavily armed oil crews panicked when they saw the Indians and opened fire. Returning the volley with spears and arrows, the Indians drove the intruders out of their homeland and then vanished into the shadows of the jungle like ghosts.

Spirits hide where spirits can, and just because a man does not see them does not mean they are not there. Through the window of his New York mansion, Nelson Rockefeller admired the perfectly manicured trees and flora of his sprawling estate while stroking the feathers on an arrow made by an Amazon tribesmen who had attacked his oil crew. He found it ironic that at the beginning of the Nuclear Age, when men first believed they had the power to destroy the world, there were still naked tribesmen with bows and arrows living along a South American river.

Up north on the Hudson River, nature had been restrained and domesticated to create a form of order that suited Rockefeller's goals, but the Amazon remained untamed, and this troubled his plans for development. Unlike his grandfather, who had shown no mercy for any obstacles that stood in the way of his progress, Nelson Rockefeller saw himself as a philanthropic humanitarian and wanted to find a nonviolent way to remove the Amazonian Indians of Peru and Venezuela from their traditional land so that drilling could begin. Rockefeller found his answer in a starry-eyed prophet named William Cameron Townsend.

Townsend was the director of the Wycliffe Bible Translators and a founder of the same Summer Institute of Linguistics that had sponsored an undercover Eunice Pike in Huautla. He had spent a decade baptizing the tribes of Mexico and Central America before Pike found out what Townsend had been after all along. Like Cortés before him, Townsend believed that the Plumed Serpent was actually the living Beast of Revelation. Although the Mazatecans corroborated Pike's story that the Plumed Serpent had been born in these mountains, there were whispers that it had departed in search of a more remote hideout.

Townsend went to Huautla to check out the situation for himself and while he was there, he dreamt of the Plumed Serpent's image carved into a sheer cliff above a thick jungle. He believed this to be a sign of the location of the beast's current hiding place. In search of the beast, Townsend followed the Plumed Serpent's trail from the Mountains of the Clouds in Mexico to South America's Amazon Jungle. When Townsend arrived in the Alto Orinoco he saw *Cerro Pintado*, an ancient petroglyph image of the feathered beast carved into the side of a jungle mountain. He immediately recognized this as the sign he had seen in his dream.

Townsend, or "Cam," as his closest followers called him, saw himself as a latter-day saint who had been chosen by God to fulfill the fundamentalist Prophecy of Two Thousand Tribes. He would be the one to end the plumed beast's reign over the Americas and bring about Cam's own version of the End of Days. In the Prophecy of Two Thousand Tribes, God views humankind as being beyond redemption and decides to purge the world of sin by destroying all life, except for a handful of chosen fundamentalists who then abandon the sins of the earth and ascend to heaven. The Prophecy of Two Thousand Tribes was the mirror opposite of the Ghost Dance since the latter, when fulfilled, would save the entire human niche in nature, not just the lives of a chosen few. The final showdown between the Ghost Dancer and the Prophecy of Two Thousand Tribes had begun.

Townsend knew that the Amazon tribes who called this region home did not trust outsiders and would never reveal the hideaway of this most sacred totem. His only choice was to begin evangelizing the local tribes until he found an informant who would betray the feathered god of their old beliefs in favor of the new Christian God. But these remote Amazon tribes had a reputation for killing male missionaries, whom they viewed as invaders. Townsend was forced to come up with an alternative means to evangelize the last remaining tribes of the Amazon.

In 1947, after years of failed attempts by male missionaries, a devout follower of Townsend named Rachel Saint became the spearhead of Townsend's crusade. Rachel and a female companion headed upriver from the jungle outpost of Shell Mera using a motorboat supplied by the Shell Oil Company. Cameron had convinced the ladies that God would protect them from the hostile, head-hunting tribes of the region because they were women doing God's work.

Their strong faith carried the women upriver into a region beyond the reach of civilization, where previously uncontacted tribes still shrank human heads as trophies. When they finally arrived at a Jivaro tribal village, the women found the chief of the village, Tariri, ghost dancing with invisible entities under a drug-induced spell.

Suffering from heat fatigue in the surreal jungle setting, Rachel Saint, like Pike before her, could see demonic ghosts that the witchdoctors had conjured flying around their feather-bedecked heads. The missionary women, with their blue eyes and pale skin as dry as dead piranhas, looked to the startled villagers like demon ghosts or witches. The Indians knew there was no point in killing these she-demons because the Lord of Witches would only send more. So the chief decided they needed to appease the Lord of Witches and allow the missionaries to stay.

Since first arriving with Columbus, missionaries had continually brought death by disease to all the tribes with whom they came in contact. Even though the missionaries themselves were completely aware of this heinous cycle, they continued on as if it were God's will. To rationalize this destruction, Saint, like many of the other missionaries, came to believe that it was the missionary's job to save souls, not lives.

Fiercely resisting evangelization more than other tribes, the still-uncontacted Huaroni had already killed Rachel Saint's brother Nate and four other naïve missionaries who had tried to evangelize them with Bibles, photographs of themselves, hamburgers and religious music. Sadly, this one incidence of violence from people who defended themselves with spears gave the civilized world an excuse to portray all Amazon tribes as murderous killers.

After her brother's death, Rachel Saint, who had picked up the tick of constantly swatting at the demons that she believed the witchdoctors had sent to attack her, became the poster child for evangelizing the fierce tribes. Stirred by her newfound fame, Saint began bringing Amazon Indians to New York City. From there the awestruck Indians, who believed they were ghost dancing through the world of the dead, were taken on a whirlwind fundraising crusade across the United States with ministers that included the famous Reverend Billy Graham. Most people had no idea there were still naked, wild tribesmen left in the world and thousands of fundamentalists gave donations to save the Indians' "heathen" souls.

But there was one donor Saint sought out above all the rest: Nelson Rockefeller, Townsend's silent partner and the man whose oil companies had the most influence over the South American governments whose countries contained parts of the Amazon Jungle. Rockefeller had come under scrutiny for using the US military to create coups in South America for his own personal gain and was looking for a way to improve his public image. So, when Saint offered him the opportunity, Rockefeller gladly obliged.

Saint portrayed Rockefeller as a benevolent humanitarian who used his philanthropic Rockefeller Foundation to fund the medical aid needed to save the tribes of the Upper Amazon. Unfortunately, by the time the aid arrived, it was too late and the already-raging epidemics had escalated far beyond the abilities of modern science to defeat.

The clock was ticking on the conversion of the Amazon Indians' souls and Townsend had to make a move before the window of opportunity closed. He decided it was time to reveal to the entire world his secret agenda, so he convinced Rockefeller to help him build a shrine to his vision.

The Two Thousand Tribes Pavilion at the 1964/1965 New York World's Fair was a cement blob that purportedly depicted an Amazonian tribal hut made of sticks and palm fronds. Inside, Cameron Townsend's uplifting voice played over a public address system. He lovingly portrayed the tribesmen of the Upper Amazon as a people deeply in need of spiritual salvation from Satan's dominion by the One True God.

Visiting his own shrine, Townsend gazed up at the murals he had commissioned. They depicted horrific images of drug-crazed witchdoctors transforming themselves into vipers. The witchdoctors surrounded their bloodthirsty Chief Tariri who was pictured cutting off his enemies' heads and shrinking them, despite there being no history of Tariri's Shapra tribe ever having engaged in the practice of head shrinking. Although the portrayal was an illusion that misrepresented reality, it was presented in a way that made it appear to be true.

The price Townsend paid in his conscience for creating this illusion was high and tore his soul apart, for in spite of their savage nature, he had grown to love the naked innocence of the tribes. Over and over again Townsend wrestled with this predicament in his mind, knowing, like the Latter-Day Saints before him, there would be blood on this road to redemption.

Finally, God gave Townsend the insight he needed to come to terms with his tortured soul. At the End of Days, all living things would be destroyed by God's wrath so there was really nothing Townsend could do to save the Amazon Indians. What he could do was save the Indians' souls before the Tribulation began. This way, both he and the tribes he loved could enter the Kingdom of Heaven together.

CHAPTER 21
THE BRAZILIAN MIRACLE

The Dog God (Xolotl)

L ove is the kingdom of heaven and so the Toltec Ghost Dancer found his way to the sensuous petal of *Xochiquetzal*. The goddess Precious Flower's essence was of blossoming flowers and she exuded the pure life force that turns a girl into a woman. Her scent intoxicated the Toltec and her touch filled him with a desire far beyond lust. Precious Flower was blooming right at the edge of innocence and just beginning to realize the power of her femininity. Although the Ghost Dancer tried to stay on the path and resist her nubile charms, he could not deny her, for this was the Petal of Eternal Joy.

Joy was not a constant state but a dance in which each step took the Ghost Dancer deeper under its spell. This romantic interplay between hunter and prey was called the Deer Dance, and never before had the Toltec felt such compelling emotions as when he deer danced with Precious Flower. It was an all-encompassing, complete infatuation with the breathtaking beauty of the young goddess.

No petal more than Precious Flower's made the Toltec Ghost Dancer yearn to be alive again. Two ghostly skeletons had found their true soul mates in the world of the dead, and the Toltec could not help but dream how wonderful it would have been to find true love in life. Even though the faded ghost of her potential was still divine, to feel her life force in all its glory would have been pure bliss.

Why and for what reason would the Toltec ever want to leave this Petal of Eternal Joy? But there is always trouble in paradise. Softened by love and tired of the constant battle to continue along the Rope of the Dead, the Ghost Dancer was no longer driven to complete the task for which he had given his life. While he enjoyed the ripening of the sweetest of fruits, his living descendants continued to suffer and he was haunted by their cries. Without a means to communicate with their ancestors, the living descendants were doomed unless the Ghost Dancer continued on his path to mend the Rope of the Dead.

Disturbed by this realization, the Toltec questioned the gods' reasons for showing him joy and then taking it away again.

"How could something that feels so good be bad for you?" he questioned. Hearing his plea, Grandfather Fire answered,

"Come close to my fire and it will keep you warm, but if you get too close it will burn you. Joy is the reason to live, but if you don't grind your edge against the hard stone of life and death, you will not have the edge needed to appreciate or defend that joy which is a gift of this goddess."

Ignoring the gods, the Toltec remained in love's embrace. He no longer wanted to face the struggle to achieve his goal. Instead, he just wanted to feel the warmth of his lover's arms. They were skeletal soul mates, ghosts in love, and they danced for no one but themselves, forgetting the tribe. They wanted the cruel world to go away, without realizing that the price the Ghost Dancer would pay would be authority over his own destiny. And so it happened.

The constant spilling of his seed weakened the Ghost Dancer until he lost his edge for survival, always seeking a deeper satisfaction that could never be fulfilled. Realizing her love could destroy his future generations, the goddess Precious Flower harangued the Ghost Dancer until he was forced to leave the warmth of her embrace and continue his journey to mend the Rope of the Dead. Only then, when authority over the land was returned to the native people, would the Toltec have Precious Flower's respect and complete devotion. So with a heavy heart the Ghost Dancer left his soul mate behind to finish the task he had undertaken.

THE VILLAS-BÔAS BROTHERS

Nelson Rockefeller convinced himself that he could take authority over the land by controlling its oil. The 1964 military coup to remove the opposing President João Goulart began the "Brazilian Miracle," Rockefeller's plan to make Brazil a modern nation by developing the natural resources of the Amazon Jungle. Turning the forest into fast money was economically sound yet environmentally shortsighted and ultimately catastrophic to the native inhabitants.

Rockefeller entrusted this job to Cameron Townsend's second in command: Eunice Pike's younger brother, Kenneth Pike. When the Indians resisted the fundamentalist missionaries' attempts to control them and change their way of life, the military intervened and convinced Kenneth Pike to enlist his followers to map out locations of villages to be used in airstrike bombings. The frightened tribesmen had never before seen fire fall from the sky and believed they had angered the missionaries' god. To end the bombing, the Indians agreed to stop attacking the oil and road crews and allow the evangelical Christians to stay. Unfortunately, shortly after the bombing ended, epidemics of disease ravaged the tribes.

Three years before, in 1961, the three Brazilian brothers Cláudio, Orlando and Leonardo Villas-Bôas had persuaded President Goulart to sign a law creating the Xingu National Park and Indigenous Peoples Preserve. The preserve was a last-ditch effort to protect the Amazon Indians from full-scale genocide. The Villas-Bôas brothers had given up comfortable lives and secure jobs in search of adventure in the jungle. Fascinated by the wild and free tribes of the Amazon, they enlisted in the military jungle corps of Colonel Cândido Rondon. Colonel Rondon's mother was of Amazon indigenous descent, and because of this, Rondon was much more sympathetic to the Indian's plight than the other military officers.

When the post-war 1950s began, Colonel Rondon received his orders from the military high command to begin to prepare the Xingu River region of the Amazon Jungle for development. It was believed the Xingu area was rich in natural resources, so the Colonel sent the Villas-Bôas brothers to build airstrips for future exploration and to document the few scattered small tribes of the Xingu River.

As the brothers scouted the region they began to make contact with more and more previously uncontacted tribes. The Xingu turned out to be a vast social network of many indigenous nations, living in a state of relative harmony despite their constant ceremonial warfare.

Living with the tribes, the brothers grew more sympathetic to the Amazonians' plight. But they still had to obey their orders, so they compromised to make the best of a difficult situation. In Brazil, shooting wild Indians on sight was still a common practice, but Colonel Rondon and the Villas-Bôas brothers came up with a new policy to never shoot an Indian, even when faced with danger. Their unbending commitment to protect the native peoples caused their legend to spread among the Indian tribes and they were welcomed where no previous outsiders had ever dared to tread. Their years spent living among the tribes prepared the brothers for the ominous events soon to unfold.

When the epidemics hit the native population, the missionaries failed to maintain medical care for the indigenous peoples. Desperate, the Villas-Bôas brothers came up with a backup plan to protect the tribes by relocating them to the preserve where they could still live close to their traditional ways. But the brothers needed to convince the skeptical tribes to leave their besieged homelands and move to the preserve.

Cláudio Villas-Bôas came to understand that the only way to gain the trust of the Indians was to earn the respect of their ancestral ghosts, so he began to take tribal sacraments and participate in their Ghost Dance ceremonies. By taking part in each of the different tribes' Ghost Dances, Cláudio was able to gain the favor of the ancestors and lead the tribes out of harm's way and onto the Xingu Preserve. No mining or development was legally allowed in the park, but there was no way to enforce the law in that regard.

After the Brazilian government allowed developers to illegally enter the preserve, Orlando Villas-Bôas used the international media to bring the tribal side of the story to the outside world. This was the beginning of the international rainforest environmental movement. In response, the Brazilian newspapers viciously attacked the third brother Leonardo for marrying a young Indian girl, portraying the brothers as opportunistic "Indian lovers" who mingled with savages. This ugly racism broke Cláudio's heart and he lost all hope that the government would keep its word. In an effort to regain his faith, he left the park and traveled from tribe to tribe searching for a medicine man who could help ensure the survival of the Amazon and its people.

Cláudio became a lone ascetic who could walk into a previously uncontacted community completely unarmed. Indians waiting in ambush lowered their bows and war clubs, slowly milling around the stranger and talking to each other in excited spurts. Cláudio would then assume the correct posture and stand perfectly still, showing no fear. He knew that the ancestral ghosts had already told the Indians that he was coming.

It was in these isolated villages that Cláudio first noticed the nature of the Plague Mother. Insects like mosquitoes, flies and gnats carried the germs which had taken over niches in nature once filled by healthy life forms. These minions of the Mother of All Plagues fed, moving and hiding much like the wild game the Indians hunted. Cláudio finally understood the nature of his enemy and picked up the scent of the epidemics, traveling deeper and deeper into the jungle where animals had never seen people before. He went to places where Mother Nature used the dense forest to keep deadly hibernating microbes away from the human herd.

Cláudio's teacher was the jungle herself, and through the sacred brew *ayahuasca*, he could now hear the voices of the plants and trees created by the rustling of the leaves. These voices spoke of the clues he searched for and led him deeper into the mystery. Cláudio had finally crossed the invisible line of Pan-American mysticism and tapped into the network the plants and ancestors used to communicate with each other.

As his awareness shifted, Cláudio became a Ghost Dancer and he no longer saw the microbes of infectious diseases as random individual germs. Instead, he began to see the epidemics through a plant's eyes: as a swarm that had unified into one living predator, the Mother of All Plagues, a predator spawned on the suffering of the tribes and which was now searching for new hosts.

When the jungle was cut down, the epidemics were released upon the rural towns and cities. These overpopulated living centers were now filled with immune-deficient people weakened by poverty, alcohol abuse, impostor corn, filth and pollution. Carried by these new human hosts, the Plague Mother's white worms hitched a ride to the urban centers on the buses that rode on the roads the developers built.

Understanding hit Cláudio Villas-Bôas like a wall of mosquitoes. He realized that pesticides and all of the Rockefeller Foundation's pharmaceutical drugs could not stop these epidemics. Only the plants who had given humans their flesh and breath of life could intercede, but the plants were not talking. So the ancestors decided to pull some strings.

THE KOGI

Inside a small stone cabin, a long-haired Kogi boy in a white, cotton robe twitched like a marionette in the spasm of spiritual possession. His eyes quivered half shut, sensing the ancestral ghosts tugging at him. Two white-robed Kogi medicine men, called *mamas*, tended to him, sitting on each side of the young man while painting their *coca* gourds with silvery saliva. The first *mama* whispered into the boy's left ear, "Sacred knowledge is kept a secret until the moment the knowledge is needed. Revealing the sacred too soon causes it to lose wisdom, but if knowledge is never used, the knowledge loses its power."

Next, the second *mama* whispered into the boy's right ear, explaining the details of the world outside the cave. Then a howling wind tore through Colombia's Sierra Nevada, bringing rain. Minutes later, the rain stopped abruptly and a tropical sun burned through the clouds, turning the sky blue once again.

The first *mama* spoke again. "All the gods of nature live on this mountain, from its snow-covered peaks to the tropical forests. Because we are a peaceful people, we have been given the responsibility of maintaining the gods' balance in the world. Each day we must make offerings at their sacred altars. But now, for the first time, the gods are worried about the *Pachamama*, the Earth Mother."

The boy, chosen by the ancestral ghosts to become a *mama*, had been placed in the small stone hut below the sacred cave where he had lived in isolation for years. This extreme solitude had altered his consciousness, but now it was time to end the ritual. For the first time in a very long time, the two *mamas* led the boy out of the stone hut and into the outside world. The boy stepped outside and squinted in the light of day and then went into a state of shock, for he saw a terrible vision. The vision scared the other *mamas* so much that the Kogi, an extremely remote and reclusive people, allowed themselves to be video-documented for the first time in 1990. As the Keepers of the Climate of the Americas, they had a desperate message for all of humanity.

In the video a Kogi *mama* says, "The world does not have to end; it could go on. But unless we stop violating the earth and nature, depleting the Great Mother of her life force, her blood, her vitality, unless people stop working against the Mother, the world will not last."

International filmmakers and activists then brought the Kogi's plea to the outside world via the internet, movies and the news. The Kogi of Colombia also shared a legend with the world, which told of the elder brothers of the Kogi who would ultimately teach the younger brothers and sisters, modern people, the proper way to live within the weave of nature. The legend was an old one and was once shared by many other tribes, including the Hopi, who learned of it from *Pahana*, and the Lakota, who were given the legend by White Buffalo Calf Woman. Though this story was inherent in the soil of the Americas, the little brothers and sisters still did not listen to the Kogi's pleas.

CHAPTER 22
THE LAST OF THE WILD AND FREE

The Earth Mother (Coatlicue)

Tezcatlipoca wanted to steal a shard of the *tiponi* back from the Kogi, but their hearts were too pure and the Lord of Witches could not trick them. Instead, the Kogi continued to ghost dance and so held on to their authority over their land. While *Tezcatlipoca's* attention was focused on the missing shards, the Toltec Ghost Dancer left Precious Flower's petal in search of the Rope of the Dead. But without the map inscribed on the *tiponi*, the Toltec strayed from his path and instead stumbled into the Forest of Lost Dreams. This was where the Moon Mother, whom the Yanomami called *Peripo-yoma*, had hidden a magical bundle of her daughter's blood. From this blood the original ancestors were created by the Yanomami's god *Omave* (their own *Quetzalcoatl*) at the first Ghost Dance.

Every morning the Moon Mother would return to mourn at her daughter's medicine bundle in the Black Flower below. Every evening, as darkness filled the night sky, the rage over her daughter's death grew within her, red as blood, and the Moon Mother would rise up in the heavens searching for the hunter who had loved and killed her daughter. Even though it was the Moon Mother's meddling that had brought tragedy down upon the star-crossed lovers, she wanted her revenge.

In the beginning when the first man appeared, the Moon Mother had convinced her young daughter, the first woman, to belittle the young hunter. The Moon Mother told her daughter that if she never acknowledged his advances, the young hunter would continue to bring them game meat in an effort to win her favor. When the hunter found out about the mother's plot, he confronted the daughter, asking for her love.

But once again following her mother's advice, instead of expressing her feelings, the daughter insulted the young hunter's manhood. Unable to bear any more insults, he flew into the jealous rage of a wild animal and shot his true love with an arrow. From then on, the Yanomami believed that it was the blood of the Moon Mother's daughter that made men into fierce defenders of the jungle.

The moon with a bellyful of red blood rose up like a mortal wound in the black and blue Amazon sky. Fearing his own mother-in-law's revenge, a naked Yanomami tribesman drew his bow and shot a seven-foot arrow at the red moon. Dripping from the moon, a drop of blood twinkled like a red star in the blackness of night, but the star he saw that night was not made of moon blood. Instead, this was a star made by the hands of men.

In 1987, a satellite launched for the Southern Hemisphere collected infrared images of an unknown waterway hidden below the canopy of the Amazon rainforest. This hidden river's source of water is in the Parima Mountain Range separating Brazil from Venezuela. During the rainy season, the run-off creates a lake in the basin on the Venezuelan side of the mountain range. Filled with all the gold and minerals that have washed down from the oldest landmass on earth, the Guiana Shield, this lake is the place the Inca knew the Spanish called El Dorado and it is here that the subterranean Tree of Life is rooted.

Airplanes cannot fly over the region in the rainy season because of the dangerous thunderhead clouds that fill the sky with electricity. During the dry season, when the clouds dissipate, the pilots still see nothing because each year the lake dries up and vanishes shortly after the rains end.

For this reason, El Dorado's gold remained undetected by the outside world for centuries, until that is, the arrival of satellite technology with infrared cameras which could see through the thick canopy of the Amazon Jungle during the heavy rains.

EL DORADO

In 1493, the legend of El Dorado, the source of the Inca's vast quantity of gold, inspired Cortés to conquer Mexico and General Pizarro to conquer South America. Though General Pizarro tortured the Inca prince Atahualpa in an attempt to determine the location of El Dorado, he was ultimately unsuccessful. Instead of giving General Pizarro the location, Atahualpa cursed the conquistador's future generations and claimed that the Inca god of coca would punish the invaders' descendants for their forefathers' brutality.

In 1987, when El Dorado was finally discovered, Atahualpa's curse had been fulfilled. Cocaine synthesized from the sacred coca leaves of an Inca god had become the most dangerous drug in the civilized world and had spun the conquerors' descendants into a toxic disco fever as the indigenous world continued to ghost dance.

Carried by the Plague Mother's breath, *xawara*, the diseases that had brought the Inca Empire to its knees five hundred years earlier had finally reached El Dorado, the golden place that had inspired the conquest. Although the Venezuelan government tried to keep out the miners who carried the diseases, they could not stop giant Canadian mining conglomerates from illegally flying Brazilian gold miners in helicopters across the remote jungle border to El Dorado.

The miners then not only polluted the rivers with mercury and filth, they kidnapped and forced Yanomami girls as young as ten years old into prostitution. When the girls became ill from the abuse, they were released and returned to their villages where they unknowingly infected their tribes with disease. A deathblow had been thrown at the end of the world among the remotest fringes of humanity and the last dying flame of *indianismo* was under attack.

Before his final Ghost Dance in Mexico, the great sage, the Old Turtle, had prophesized that the last Witches War of this One Reed Cycle of the Ghost Dance would be fought at El Dorado in the Great Jungle of the South. And so it was said that the battle to save the human niche in the weave of nature would be fought where the subterranean Tree of Life grew, in the Alto

Orinoco of Venezuela. This was also believed to be the home of the last previously uncontacted tribes in the world.

Burning funeral pyres as abundant as the stars in the sky filled the jungle with the scent of burnt flesh. All the way up to the River of the Blue Parakeets, the cries of wailing women blended with the buzzing of the swarms of flies which gathered on the half-decayed corpses of loved ones, hanging from trees like strange rotting fruit. There were so many corpses that the sick Indians could not cremate them all, so they hung the bodies in the trees to protect them from scavenging animals. The Mother of All Plague's white worms of disease had finally arrived at El Dorado.

On the banks of the Alto Ocamo River of Venezuela, a Yanomami woman fell to the ground and shook in spasms until her fellow tribesmen believed she was dead. Hours later, the woman appeared to come back to life and began to ghost dance, swaying in a trance while singing to the ancestors, "I saw the eyes of all my dead relations and I danced with them so the *xawara* won't kill us all."

All through the Alto Orinoco region of the Amazon rainforest, the Yanomami began following the woman in the steps of her Ghost Dance, crying for their lost loved ones while rocking back and forth. Then they washed their bodies with earth to cleanse them of the foul smell of the *xawara* and chanted.

"Your brother *Omave* has traveled far and brought back the outsiders' *xawara*. Help us, *Yomave*, Lord of Witches, to break its deadly spell."

For the Yanomami, *Omave's* civilization had brought disease. Only *Tezcatlipoca*, the Lord of Witches, whom the Yanomami called *Yomave*, could stop the death wails. When the Lord of Witches heard their mournful prayers, he appeared from the smoke rising from a medicine man's corpse on a smoldering pyre and proceeded to consume the bones of their dead. This was his way of once again becoming one with the tribe.

After the Yanomami's dead were cremated, the women collected the charred bones, ground them into ash and sprinkled the ashes into a bark canoe-shaped vessel filled with a mashed banana drink. The Yanomami cremated their dead and drank their ashes so the ancestral ghosts could live on within their bodies, forever part of the tribe. To commemorate this continuing cycle of life, the women mixed some of the ashes of their dead relatives with tears and painted the black paste onto their cheeks. Their mourning period ended when the paste dried and flaked off. This was a pure, primordial form of the Ghost Dance, as the Yanomami danced with the ghosts of their dead who lived inside them.

While the Yanomami ghost danced, one of their most revered medicine men had a vision sent to him by the Lord of Witches. *Yomave* showed the medicine man how to rid the Yanomami of the miners by using the power of illusion. At sunset, hidden in a forest glade above the gold fields, the medicine man snorted his *epene* snuff and began to dance and sing, inviting all the forest's *hekura*, animal spirits, and *xapori*, human ghosts, into his spirit house. His spirit house was the medicine man's body, with the ribs as the roof and the spine as the center pole. After the old man danced and sang for a long time, billows of white luminescence appeared, floating around him like tiny clouds.

As his vision began, the little clouds became the downy hair on the heads of the luminous *xapori* all lined up in a kaleidoscope of mirrored images. One by one, they followed the scent of *epene* snuff, a favorite food, into the spirit house of the old medicine man's chest.

The Spider Mother *hekura* became the central deity in the spirit house and as the medicine man danced, *Ocello* Spider, the Mother of Weavers, descended on one single strand of a web. The more the medicine man sang and danced in the world of the living, the more spiders descended and made webs, until the entire gold field had been hidden. After the medicine man's ceremony, the miners no longer found gold and they left El Dorado believing that the hidden gold fields had dried up.

Once again, a medicine man with ancestral spirits, the *xapori*, had come to the Yanomami's defense, bringing the people of the forest a moment's reprieve from the onslaught of the outside world. But the monumental ceremony took all the old medicine man's strength and left him tired and drained, so he left the Parima and returned to the Alto Ocamo where his tribe was burning the corpses of the dead in huge funeral pyres. The Pashopicowe-ateri Yanomami cried over the bones of their loved ones and sang to the sky, asking for an omen of what was to become of them.

Like a giant prehistoric insect, a Eurocopter AS 332L1 Super Puma helicopter flew out of the thunderhead, following the procession of the Ghost Dancer's funeral pyres up the Alto Ocamo to the River of the Blue Parakeets in the Siapa River Basin. From below the jungle's canopy, the Yanomami Ghost Dancers swayed back and forth with their arms raised over their heads. They believed that the helicopter was a foreign witch's giant dragonfly *hekura* whose toxic fumes of *xawara* had caused the dreaded epidemics.

The helicopter carrying the ill-fated Foundation to Aid Peasant and Indigenous Families (FUNDAFACI) expedition entered the Siapa River Basin. They thought the basin was the last place left on earth where there were still truly uncontacted tribes. The stated purpose of the expedition was to assess and bring medical aid to these last tribal peoples who were dying from the epidemics, but there was no outreach medical team attached to FUNDAFACI until after the expeditions had begun. The medical aspect was only a cover-up for the true purpose of the expedition.

Four months earlier, the mistress of Venezuelan President Carlos Andrés Pérez had convinced him, during pillow talk, to inaugurate the Alto Orinoco Tapiripoca Biosphere Reserve. The biosphere reserve would be the largest protectorate of flora, fauna and indigenous people in the Americas and would supposedly help the besieged Yanomami.

But immediately after the reserve was opened, Jim Boe, the head of the evangelical Christian New Tribes Mission in Venezuela, used his clout with the oil companies to take control of the reserve's board of directors. This was not just happenstance; Boe believed that the Yanomami were the last tribe needed to fulfill the Prophecy of Two Thousand Tribes.

Wanting to fulfill her own destiny, the Venezuelan president's mistress, Cecilia Matos, quickly changed her colors from gold to environmental green. Her backroom partner, the Venezuelan gold miner and explorer Charlie Brewer-Carías, had convinced her that the riches of El Dorado could be theirs if they just removed the missionaries and the other gold miners.

Matos' boyfriend, President Pérez, could not eliminate her enemies but he did make a move. In 2002 he began backing Matos' instant charity organization: FUNDAFACI.

FUNDAFACI was created as a foundation which would protect peasants and indigenous people, but Matos' secret plan was to use the foundation's expeditions to not only search for gold but also to expose Jim Boe, the head of the New Tribes Mission. Boe was a notorious pedophile and Matos wanted to use his inappropriate behavior to have all of the missionaries removed, so she could be the new "Queen of El Dorado."

Touching down at a remote jungle village, Matos never left her helicopter. Instead, she was photographed dressed in a designer safari outfit, throwing unusable gifts to the Yanomami. Then she quickly headed back to the arms of President Pérez in Caracas to get money for more expeditions and to have her picture plastered all over the society columns in the newspapers. 'Jungle Cecilia' had become an environmental celebrity who would soon be featured at the coming Earth Summit in Rio de Janeiro. But the truth was, she loved only gold.

A month after Matos' jungle visit, the president's Super Puma helicopter once again carried the FUNDAFACI expedition to one of the most remote places on earth. This time, when the door of the helicopter opened at the village of Ashetowe-ateri, Matos' partner, Charlie Brewer-Carías, stepped out of the Age of Technology and into the so-called Stone Age. Upon his arrival, the scared inhabitants of Ashetowe-ateri were too sick to attack the flying demon that expelled the *xawara* fumes of disease. But to determine whether the giant dragonfly was male or female, a brave villager inspected the underbelly of the helicopter and deducted that it was female because he mistook the people coming out of its side for white larvae. Only when they saw Napoleon Chagnon, the man who had made the Yanomami infamous as "The Fierce People," urinate, did the Yanomami understand that the giant white larvae were humans.

Then, for a brief moment, interaction between the indigenous and modern worlds was actually successful as the scouts brought in badly needed game food with their shotguns and the doctors of the Parima Culebra medical group began to work on patients. A shotgun and modern science appeared to bring Ashetowe-ateri back from the claws of the *xawara's* death grip, and for the first time in a long time, the women began to dance and sing. Doctors of Parima Culebra and other members of the expedition joined in and a deep joy came over the village. In spite of the expedition leaders' misconduct, something magical had happened at the edge of the world. Although the outsiders could not see it, the dance and songs called the *xapori* out of the jungle and into these medicine men's spirit houses to dance with their descendants.

Within days, rumors of illegal gold exploration began to pour out of the jungle and a military helicopter was sent to bring the FUNDAFACI expedition back to the capital of Caracas. When the helicopter arrived at Ashetowe-ateri, Brewer-Carías ordered it to land in the village plaza so it could pick up his heavy, mysterious cargo. While landing, the helicopter accidentally knocked down the roof of the *xapono* communal hut which then fell on a half dozen people and scattered the ashes of the Yanomami's ancestors to the wind. Once again it was the *xawara* wind of a metal machine that blew away the good relations needed to truly fight an epidemic. The effort to save the last intact tribal nation on earth had been bought and sold before it ever began.

When the helicopter landed at La Carlota Airport in Caracas, FUNDAFACI's pedophile trump card to remove the New Tribes Mission became second page news to Lieutenant Colonel Hugo Chávez's military coup. Chávez and his colleagues were infuriated by President Pérez's greedy exploitation of Venezuela's natural resources. Pérez had allowed his mistress and her gold-mining cronies to play as they pleased in the fields of the lord while the Indians suffered at their expense. Chávez and the other lower class, mid-level officers had purposely picked the day the FUNDAFACI expedition returned to Caracas to make their daring move.

By the next morning, Chávez's coup attempt had failed and he was escorted to a military prison. With Matos and Brewer-Carías embroiled in political intrigue in the city, the New Tribes Mission remained in control of El Dorado, like a fox watching over a chicken coop.

As the millennium came to an end, Jim Boe, the head of the New Tribes Mission, believed that the time to fulfill the prophecy had arrived. Once the Yanomami, the last wild and free tribe, were evangelized, there would be no one left to believe in the Plumed Serpent and, without believers, the biblical beast would no longer exist.

CHAPTER 23
THE PROPHECY OF TWO THOUSAND TRIBES

The Rain God (Tloloc Sequah)

W hen two Clean Sisters meet, they lay their *reboso* shawls over their arms in a special way and gently touch fingers, letting the other know that they are with another of the sisterhood.

One by one, thirteen demure ladies dressed in *huipils* embroidered with hummingbirds and flowers entered a weathered but impeccably maintained shack. After greeting each other with a *"Dali de tin de,"* they took their seats on straw mats in front of a rustic altar with a picture of Mary Magdalene enshrined with wildflowers and a beeswax candle.

"Grandfather Fire," they sang, "it is your loving granddaughters who seek your blessing. We are Eagle Women and Moon Sisters. We helped write Precious Flower's sacred book. We are the daughters of María Magdalena and the caretakers of both the Ghost Dancers and our beloved patron *nagual* who has left us to go hide in the Great Jungle of the South."

Then the Clean Sisterhood stopped singing and an elder sister spoke. "The Sisterhood senses the time has come and our precious patron is being surrounded by demons. As this calendar cycle comes to an end, we wish to send a message down into the Black Flower asking the Mistress of the Dead to release the spirits of the Ghost Dancers who are Mother Nature's warriors."

The elder Sister lit copal incense and then began to chant as she moved pairs of Little Ones through the incense smoke.

"Grandfather Fire, we do not ask for ourselves but call upon you to help the tribe of humankind, for now is the time we need our Grandfather the most. We ask you to call upon the gods in humanity's defense, for without them the Plumed Serpent's children are lost."

After chanting, each sister ate seven pairs of the Little Ones and then the eldest blew out the candle. As the light faded from the world of the living, one last sliver of Grandfather's flame pierced the earth and, for a brief moment, continued to shine in the underworld.

By that fading light the Toltec ghost could see the faint glimmer of the Pool of Origins off in the distance. He knew now that he had finally arrived at the place of his destiny, where the torn Rope of the Dead hung from the Tree of Life, which had grown from *Tezcatlipoca's* severed foot.

Excited by the joy of arrival, the Toltec blindly rushed towards the Tree, but as he reached towards the pool his bony knees buckled, overcome by the stench of the Plague Mother's foul *xawara* breath. Before he could get his balance, the Ghost Dancer was covered in the Plague Mother's white worms and he was overcome with fear. But then the voice of plants spoke from the darkness.

"So stand up and free yourself, Ghost Dancer. Can't you see that you've been tricked by your own fear? The Plague Mother's worms cannot hurt a skeletal ghost because you have no flesh or organs to feed upon."

Hearing these words of encouragement made the Toltec feel brave and he rattled his bones, shaking off the white worms that had shrouded him. As he regained his courage, he watched as a brilliant-blue butterfly emerged from the darkness.

VOICES FROM THE PAST

Hugo Chávez awoke from a worm-infested nightmare to see a blue morpho butterfly fluttering outside his window. For him, this was no ordinary butterfly but rather a sign from his role model, the liberator Simón Bolívar, telling him it was time to stand up and face his fears. Shortly after being freed from prison, Hugo Chávez had become the president of Venezuela in a landslide victory. Although the people had elected him, it was the ancestral ghost that had chosen him as a warrior to defend the withered Tree of Life.

With the election behind him, Chávez rose to the occasion and claimed his revolutionary pedigree through his great-grandfather, the rebel leader known as Maisanta. Chávez also drew inspiration from his indigenous ancestry through his grandmother, a member of the Puna tribe. Hugo Chávez, born from the fertile soil of the Americas, was truly a son of this land. He embodied the classic struggle of Latin America's indigenous, African and European mixed identity.

President Chávez began his dance by poking a hole in the Lord of Witches' illusion and publically denounced Columbus Day as a holiday celebrating genocidal murderers. Chávez went on to drive the point of the indigenous spear deeper by changing the day into a celebration of Native American heroes, like Altahualpa, the Inca Tupac, Sitting Bull and Venezuela's own great chiefs, Caballero and Guaicaipuro.

After using Columbus Day to demonstrate that he would not be a puppet of the oligarchy, the powers that be in the Americas took notice. Chávez announced a mammoth oil strike along the Orinoco River so huge it had the potential to make Venezuela the number one oil-rich country in the world. President Chávez made it clear the revenue would be used to bring a better life to Venezuela's poor and indigenous population instead of ending up in off-shore Wall Street bank accounts.

That's when the oligarchy took action and turned to subversion. They used the media to create an illusion worthy of Tezcatlipoca and portrayed Chávez as a monster. Then the oligarchy cut off food supplies to strangle the poor back into submission. At the same time, thugs were paid to create violent chaos in the hope of destabilizing the Chávez government. The

Venezuelan oligarchy did not like anyone giving "their" oil away and Hugo Chávez became a marked man.

Ironically, oil, the substance that had led to so much destruction for the Pan-American indigenous people and their land, was now supposed to save them. No matter how much Chávez believed he could help the people, sooner or later it was inevitable that he would have to look into *Tezcatlipoca's* Mirror of Illusion and face this contradiction. When the freight train of the urban Bolivarian socialist revolution collided with the rural Indian Revival, which revolution would take precedence? Would it be more jobs for the urban poor or rights and environmental protection of flora, fauna and native peoples? Was Chávez seeing the world through the eyes of the Kogi *mamas* and dancing with the ghost of Simón Bolívar or was he just another product of the European Industrial Revolution dressed up to look indigenous?

In 2002, with one hundred million dollars stolen from the Venezuelan people, exiled ex-president Pérez launched a coup backed by the CIA to assassinate president Chávez. Military troops loyal to Chávez rescued him a moment before the assassins arrived in a Black Hawk helicopter to finish the job. When his hood was removed, Hugo Chávez was disoriented, but the first words out of his mouth were, "The *Popol Vuh*, I just kept thinking about the *Popol Vuh*."

The *Popol Vuh* was an ancient Mayan holy book based on the Ghost Dance that told the story of the journey of two ghostly brothers through the Land of the Dead. Hugo Chávez had just taken his own journey back through death's door, and inspired now by the ancestors, he began to fight to save the Tree of Life. Showing his solidarity with the indigenous struggle, Chávez proclaimed that the last intact Indian nation on earth, the Yanomami, would become Venezuela's symbol of the undying spirit of the American Indian people.

To help the Yanomami, who were dying from epidemics brought by missionaries and gold miners, Chávez created the first government-run medical projects designed specifically for the tribe. He called together all the different groups of medics, missionaries and anthropologists, including the New Tribes Mission, to work as a group towards finding a solution to the epidemic crisis.

The participation of the New Tribes Mission was crucial because they had the only airstrips and refrigerators in the region and these were needed to transport medicines safely. But the New Tribes Mission was reluctant to get involved with a medical project, as it continued to believe that missionaries were in the region to save souls, not lives. Pressured by President Chávez, the New Tribes Mission's leader, Jim Boe, eventually agreed to take part under the condition that he could choose the project's coordinator.

Boe's choice was the group known as the Tribal Outreach Medical Assistance, or TOMA. TOMA was a foundation run by the North American children of one of the New Tribes Mission's elders and had offered medical aid to the few converted tribes in the region.

Flying over the Orinoco River as it snaked through the green jungle, an Airbus cargo plane brought the TOMA expedition past the Tree of Life and up towards the mission at Parima B. In the jungle below, the vectors carrying the epidemics had finally overtaken the Yanomami. Now their only hope was to leave the big river of the bottomland with its marauding insect swarm and return to their high-altitude ancestral homeland where the mosquitoes could not survive. The Yanomami had never known the Plague Mother's diseases of malaria, dengue or yellow fever until they had come down to the big river to acquire trade goods from the first New Tribes Mission missionaries.

The fat-bellied Airbus that carried the TOMA medical relief project team landed at the same time as the sickly Yanomami refugees started to arrive from the bottomland. An ancient culture and the modern world came together at Parima B as the TOMA medics unloaded their precious medicines from the plane. Dressed in a soccer uniform three sizes too large, Brother Diego, one of the few evangelized Yanomami, and his "sunglasses posse" of enforcers, took the refugees' bows and arrows away from them.

Stripped of their weapons and ready to do anything to get the magic medicine, the refugees allowed themselves to be herded into a filthy tropical slum.

Overcome by how much their homeland had been changed by the missionaries, one of the elderly medicine men took out his *mokohiro* pipe and began to ghost dance in front of the razor wire that encircled the slum. He was calling his ancestors and the *xapori* spirits who had once protected his homeland to help his people. As he danced, a blue morpho butterfly appeared, and both the refugees and the TOMA medics watched it flutter by with wonder.

In a fit of rage brought on by his hatred of the old ways, Diego swatted at the butterfly and began to beat the elderly medicine man for performing the Yanomami Ghost Dance. When he was finished, Diego grabbed a bag of Fruit Loops that his posse were munching from and threw handfuls of the cereal at the starving refugees.

As the Yanomami scrambled for the scraps of food, Diego explained that only those who would accept Jesus as their Savior would get the magic medicine. The non-believers would have to leave and return to the disease-infested bottomland from which they had just retreated. When no one stepped forward to be baptized, Diego became angry and began to rant.

"Listen to me, stupid Indians, this is no longer the time of our grandfathers and fathers when we hunted, fished, and worshipped the devil like this sinner medicine man. We don't want the devil here. Now we have Jesus and instead of hunting, we eat sardines from a can and enjoy Fruit Loops!"

Fearing for their lives, the confused refugees lined up in front of Diego, ready to be baptized. After decades of failed evangelization, the epidemic finally succeeded where mortal man had failed.

The military pilots of the Airbus who had been watching this scene unfold were appalled. When they returned to the capital city of Caracas and reported back to President Chávez, they told him that the missionaries at Parima B were using fear tactics and the threat of disease to convert the Yanomami. There were also rumors of Jim Boe's serial pedophilia coupled with treacherous allegations that the missionaries planned to sacrifice the Yanomami to usher in the Prophecy of Two Thousand Tribes. Wasting no time, President Chávez sent a squadron of helicopters to deal with the situation at Parima B.

For the first time since the Yanomami could remember, it had stopped raining and the jungle was dying. The climate had changed and the weather no longer favored the tribes. The people wondered if this was because they had abandoned their gods for the missionaries' One True God.

A rumbling in the sky scared the Yanomami at Parima B into believing the heavens were falling. As the Yanomami watched the sky, three military helicopters appeared like a vision on the horizon. After landing, soldiers in full dress uniform exited the aircraft with flags, banners and other symbols of state. With his general's oak leaves and brass glistening in the midday sun, Hugo Chávez, the man the ancestral ghost put in charge of saving the

Tree of Life, made his move to stop the fulfillment of the Prophecy of Two Thousand Tribes.

The soldiers first lined up all the missionaries and foreigners against the razor-wire fence. Then, a mulatto officer in a red beret stepped forward and asked who was in charge. A young missionary replied, stating that he was the newly appointed leader of the New Tribes Mission at Parima B. The officer addressed the man in a formal manner, telling him that the New Tribes Mission's behavior towards the Yanomami was dangerous and disrespectful, and that the President of Venezuela had ordered them to leave.

Over the next three months, Chávez and the military closed down all the fundamentalist and evangelical Christian missions in Indian territories. The New Tribes Mission's goal of fulfilling the End of Days prophecy at El Dorado had failed.

Though badly battered, the Tree of Life and the Yanomami, Keepers of the Flame, were barely alive. Still flickering in the wind as the Plumed Serpent, the Spirit of the Americas rose up, ready to fly again.

CHAPTER 24
THE CONDOR PASSES

Lord of Witches (Tezcatlipoca)

The sacred condor flew over the Forest of Lost Dreams as the Toltec ghost finally arrived at the Pool of Origins. There, hanging from the withered, subterranean Tree of Life was the frayed end of the Rope of the Dead. The skeletal Toltec ghost squatted down and began to collect each strand of the sacred rope.

Ever so carefully, he wove the strands together, mending the lines of communication between plants, the gods, dead ancestors and living tribes. For the first time since the Toltec Empire fell, the tattered ends of the Rope of the Dead were woven together.

But the Plague Mother was not really interested in this rope or any other part of the dead, since her white worms only fed on the living. The Mother of All Plagues had never wanted to completely eradicate the Two-Legged Ones; she just wanted to cull the herd to maintain a human source for her minions to feed upon. Crafty by nature, the Plague Mother came up with a devious plan to seduce the salacious rain god *Tloloc Sequah*. She hated him for wanting to control her, and she schemed to leave him impotent and unable to use his power. Without the rain, the only one who had the knowledge to stop her plagues, *Desheto*, would die.

So the Mother of All Plagues left the underworld for the Mountains of the Clouds and as she rose up through the Vision Serpent's throat, her festering exterior was transformed and she became a radiant goddess. The Plague Mother had great skill at manipulating men and so she lured *Tloloc Sequah* to her den in the Black Flower. Exalting in her feminine charms, she consumed his time with sexual favors, draining the god of his life force and ultimately stopping the rain. What happened below happened above as well, and in South America, a conflict began to grow over water.

EVO MORALES

By 2003, the drought had spread across South America and was rapidly sucking the life force out of the high mountain plateaus of Bolivia, leaving the native population dying of thirst. In response, the government came up with a plan to help bring clean drinking water to more people. Capitalizing on the recently adopted South American version of NAFTA, the Free Trade Agreement of the Americas (FTAA), the Bolivian president granted all the water rights of the country to the Bechtel Corporation, a multinational construction and civil engineering company based in San Francisco, California.

Bechtel took control of the country's reservoirs and set up a network of pumps to supply water to Betchel's new FTAA-approved industrial farms. The Indians were allowed to connect to the system for the equivalent of $324 US dollars, a one-time fee, but one which most of them could not afford. So Bechtel turned off the faucet. When the natives tried to collect water from the dwindling rivers they were often arrested, beaten and murdered by the military units the government sent to protect Bechtel's water rights. The Aymara and Quechua Tribes no longer had the right to use the water of their ancestral lands.

Desperate, with their children literally dying of thirst, a group of Ayamara and Quechua women marched down from the Altiplano Plateau in protest. Even if their conscious minds had forgotten, these Clean Sisters were still connected to the sacred lineage of their sisterhood.

These little Indian ladies wore colonial *pollero* dresses, embroidered shawls and European bowler derbies as they marched down the mountain in search of justice. Outside the high-mountain city of Cochabamba, the ladies' ranks grew as they approached a military roadblock. Within minutes, eighty-six unarmed Indian women were shot down in cold blood by the troops and the remaining sisters ran and hid in the forest, waiting for a sign.

When Clean Sisters die, the Mother cries for them, and so for the first time in months, it began to drizzle. Those tears washed the blood of the Clean Sisters back into their mother's womb and the ladies who survived the massacre slowly emerged from the folds of the forest. Outside of Cochabamba they stood on the road, silently containing their fear of what was to come. If necessary, these women were ready to die for their children's right to live.

Just down the winding mountain road, the soldiers were lined up with their rifles pointed at the unarmed sisters, but the modest ladies would not turn back and a bloodbath once again seemed imminent. Clutching their children, the sisters' nostrils flared in readiness as they reached the soldiers blocking the road. Once again, the generals ordered the noncommissioned officers to ready their troops to fire. For a moment, time seemed to freeze in the frigid mountain air of Bolivia's Altiplano.

Only when a condor swooped down and cut through the mist did time begin again. The condor's passing had transformed the moment and one could see this realization in the officers in charge of the roadblock. Indians themselves, they couldn't give the order to open fire on women who looked just like their own mothers and sisters. By defying orders, once again, the mid-level officers could have been court-martialed, but still they chose not to shoot.

Just as the Old Turtle had predicted, it was the mid-level officers who had refused to give the order to fire upon the unarmed Indians in Chiapas, Mexico, in Venezuela, and now here in Bolivia. The brave ladies were allowed to continue on their way towards the capital of La Paz in protest. With no food or water, the poor Indian women chewed their traditional sacrament, vitamin-rich coca leaves, which sustained them. This sacred plant stood by them every inch of the way.

All night the Ayamara *amautas* (or medicine men) danced in front of the sacred Gateway of the Sun at the ruins of Tiahuanaco until a condor appeared, circling above. This huge bird, which soars higher than any other, had been the spirit animal of the Aymara since time began. After the condor vanished into the clouds, an Aymara Indian named Evo Morales stepped out of the morning mist on the road outside of Cochabamba. Morales, the president of the coca-pickers union, had been introduced to the Spiderwoman Weavers Sisterhood by his sister, who was one of the protesters. With sculpted features, a mop of black hair, sensitive eyes and broad nostrils, his features reflected the face of Bolivia.

Juan Evo Morales Ayma was a poor, moderately literate Indian himself, but he had the skills to organize the protest march and raise it to a more political level. He added his coca pickers to the gathering multitude, and by the time the Spiderwoman Weavers Sisterhood and the coca pickers union reached the Bolivian capital of La Paz, they were a million strong. Taking back their country, the protesters forced the president to resign. Then, Evo Morales turned the water faucet back on.

For the first time in the history of South America, an indigenous person had been democratically elected as the president of the Republic of Bolivia, a country with a largely indigenous population. Before Morales' official acceptance speech, Hugo Chávez joined the new president of Bolivia at a ceremony at the ruins of Tiahuanaco. There, Morales was cleansed in a traditional Aymara ceremony performed by the *amautas*.

The ceremony was held at the Gateway of the Sun, the entrance to the ruins of Tiahuanaco. This was the place the Aymara believed *Kon Tiki Viracocha*, the Aymara version of *Quetzalcoatl*, would return to fulfill the Aymara's Seven Generations Prophecy. Mostly on foot, fifty thousand Indians arrived to share in the celebration.

Although non-indigenous people like Subcomandante Marcos and mixed-bloods like Chávez had given so much to the cause, it was not until Evo Morales arrived on the scene that the Pan-American Indian Revival and its indigenous philosophy were fully embodied in the flesh.

CHAPTER 25
THE VANISHING SHADOWS OF THE FOREST

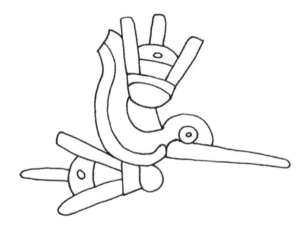

Sacred Hummingbird

While the Toltec Ghost Dancer was mending the Rope of the Dead, the ancestors came to him and said that *Desheto* was dying. Without rain *Desheto* would not survive, and without his Fruit of Knowledge, humans would never learn to communicate with the plants and find the wisdom needed to survive the Fifth World. Knowing that the rope would lose its purpose if *Desheto* died, the Toltec stopped before he had completed weaving the Rope of the Dead and rushed to help the Prince of Plants.

Searching for the rain, the Toltec arrived at the petal where the Plague Mother held the rain god *Tloloc Sequah* captive with her womanly ways. While the Plague Mother was away feeding her minions, the Toltec ghost had a chance to speak privately with *Tloloc Sequah*. The Ghost Dancer was determined to convince the temperamental rain god to leave the Plague Mother's den of iniquity and bring back the rain to save *Desheto*.

But *Tloloc Sequah* had been mesmerized by the love of love and the more he received, the more he wanted. Insatiable in his desires, it appeared there was nothing the Toltec could do or say to break the Plague Mother's lascivious spell on *Tloloc Sequah*. Luckily, true friendship was highly prized by the gods, and the rain and the wind were the ancient traveling companions of *Desheto*. By continually questioning the rain god's loyalty to his old friend, the Toltec eventually broke the Plague Mother's love spell.

When *Tloloc Sequah* realized the Plague Mother's deceit, he grew furious and agreed to help. Turning himself into a cloud, the rain god escaped the Plague Mother's petal unnoticed. Like a thief in the night, *Tloloc Sequah* rose in the heavens to return to the Seven Caves in the Mountains of the Clouds.

Having convinced the rain god to return home and help *Desheto*, the Toltec finally transformed into a true Ghost Dancer, for he had learned the divine skill of how to petition the gods. With this task behind him, the Toltec Ghost Dancer returned to the Pool of Origins to finish mending the Rope of the Dead. But when he arrived at the pool he found his nemesis, *Tezcatlipoca*, kneeling in front of the withered Tree of Life. Before the Ghost Dancer could retreat, *Quetzalcoatl* came up behind him and placed his hand on the Toltec's shoulder.

"He is not the enemy," *Quetzalcoatl* said. "My brother has struggled harder than any god to protect our Mother. I know that you thought he was out to destroy you, but that was the illusion he used in order to teach you the lessons needed to transform *Desheto*'s knowledge into wisdom. It was *Tezcatlipoca*, not I, who made you a true Ghost Dancer."

Seeing *Tezcatlipoca* as his teacher instead of his antagonist was a difficult transition to make and the Ghost Dancer looked into *Tezcatlipoca*'s eyes for confirmation of *Quetzocoatl*'s words. To the Toltec's surprise, what he saw there was not hatred but a deep concern. So the Toltec felt compassion for this god who had watched over the Two-Legged Ones everyday while the other gods remained aloof from the human struggle.

Quetzalcoatl was right; *Tezcatlipoca* was not the villain but the exalted one, the Lord of Days, and from his severed foot the Tree of Life had grown. Without *Tezcatlipoca*, humans would never have been created and instead there would only have been gods populating the Fifth World.

"Let go of your past, Ghost Dancer," *Tezcatlipoca* whispered, "so you can tie the final knot and be tethered to the gods for eternity. Is that not the blessing of a Ghost Dancer?"

Kneeling down beside the Lord of Days, the Toltec held the Rope of the Dead and very carefully mended every fiber, one by one, until *Quetzalcoatl* stopped him before he finished the very last one, saying, "Leave the last one undone, for it will bind you to us, Ghost Dancer."

The Ghost Dancer let go of the last fiber and *Tezcatlipoca* questioned him. "You, who have known *Desheto*, danced with the ancestors and learned the wisdom of the gods, have we or have we not taught my brother's children, your descendants, to see? I ask you knowing that the most dangerous destroyers of nature often portray themselves as her protectors."

A RIGGED GAME

As the Ghost Dance cycle of the calendar approached its end, a wave of social reform rolled across Latin America. After years of persecution, there was now hope that the time to hear the voice of the poor had arrived and the people believed that Luiz Inácio Lula da Silva, President of Brazil, was that voice. Lula had won the Brazilian presidential election by promising to break a centuries-long stranglehold that the international industrialists had had on the country's resources. But to fulfill his promises, Lula needed a way to bring energy resources to the rapidly growing urban masses that had supported him in the election. Unfortunately for the rainforest and the tribes who lived under its canopy, the new people's government turned to the Amazon for the raw energy it needed to power the cities.

Caught up in the grandiosity of his illusion, Lula lit the match and the Brazilian people danced the samba while half of the Amazon Jungle burned. Under the remnants of *Tezcatlipoca's* veil, Lula portrayed himself as an environmental champion who would protect the other half of the Amazon rainforest with funding created by burning down the first half. It turned out that the people's candidate was not Mother Earth's candidate.

Lula was an urban man who did not understand that there was a profound difference between the land São Paulo was built on and the Amazon Jungle. If the forests are torn down to build a New York City, São Paulo or Caracas, the earth may become more polluted, but it will survive. But if humans try to destroy the Amazon Jungle, Mother Nature's immune system, she will defend herself by purging her body of those two-legged parasites.

Setting the jungle ablaze, the new Brazilian government achieved in twelve years what the colonialists and industrialists had not managed in five hundred. The jungle fell as the fires burned at a rate never before seen, consuming in hours what had taken the Mother thousands of years to create. Many inhabitants of the forest, both two- and four-legged, died in fires that sent endless black clouds of smoke billowing up into the air and irritated the eyes of the furious gods. They watched as the spirit houses of the vaporous *xapori* crumbled and melted like slivers of ice.

The spirits of the forest leapt from shadow to shadow with blazing manes to escape the tropical inferno. Still smoldering, the forest spirits crossed over the Parima Mountain Range that separates Venezuela from Brazil, trying to find a safe haven in which to hide. On the other side of the mountain, in El Dorado, there were no flames, because Hugo Chávez had protected the Tree of Life in ex-president Perez's Alto Orinoco Biosphere Reserve.

Although many Yanomami had been evangelized in the previous year, there were still those among them who could see the beautiful *hekura* and *xapori* in the old way. Following the fleeing *hekura*, an exodus of animals moved across the border to where the subterranean Tree of Life was rooted. There, huddled together around the tree, the *xapori* held council, telling the *hekura*, the animals and the native people that this was where they were going to make their stand against the enemy of their Mother.

Vibrant radiance illuminated the *xapori's* vaporous bodies as they danced upon the Tree of Life, leaving behind trails of smoke from where they had been burned. The smoke trails swirled, hanging down into the Black Flower. As the strands of smoke reached the Toltec Ghost Dancer, he attached their ends to the Rope of the Dead and completed his sacred task.

Tezcatlipoca spoke to him. "Blessed Child of my Brother, you have come to the end of the Rope. You have survived the journey of the dead and danced with their ghosts. Now that you have completed your task, it is time for me to complete mine and tear a hole in the illusion I created."

Changing himself into a raven, *Tezcatlipoca* left the Pool of Origins for another petal where the souls of animals were kept. Turning from a raven back into the Lord of Witches, *Tezcatlipoca* studied the drawings on the wall. He was looking for one particular type of animal, a giant that had been blessed by the gods and that was so sacred, it could not get cancer like most other animals could.

To find this sacred animal, the Lord of Witches called upon White Buffalo Calf Woman. They both knew that the moment she had described to the Lakota so long ago was about to arrive. The Shepherd who guards the souls of animals lit a stick of resin wood as a torch and White Buffalo Calf Woman, the very embodiment of the Northern Clean Sisterhood, danced and sang with such feeling and grace that even the pictures on the wall began to move. Then, with huffs and snorts, the spirits of the *Tehenshela* buffalo appeared and moved through the herd images on the wall. The buffalo rubbed against each other as they became more agitated, until the thunder of their hooves was too much to bear and the Little Buffalo were vomited up out of the mouth of the Vision Serpent into the land of the living.

GRANDPA ROY

In the eyes of the gods there are no borders. Men, not the gods, had made the borders that separate the Americas into different countries. The cosmology of the Americas has always been the same, inherent in the soil with the first ritual radiating north and south, east and west, from the Mountains of the Clouds where the Ghost Dance had begun.

Far from the Mountains of the Clouds and the sweltering heat of the Amazon Jungle, eight Lakota men sang together in a steam-filled sweat lodge on the frozen back forty of the Rosebud Indian Reservation in South Dakota. Many proudly wore the scars of the Sun Dance upon their chests and the pain of a hard life in their eyes.

That night, as the vaporous ghosts of the Little Buffalo appeared in the steamy shadows of the sweat lodge, Grandpa Roy Stone wiped his brow and whispered for the blanket that served as a door to be raised. The misty visions of buffalo quickly faded into the blackness of night as Grandpa Roy crawled out of the short, round, blanket-covered sweat lodge, which represented the belly of a great buffalo.

Early the next morning, two cattle cars filled with small buffalo arrived on the Upper Brulé Sioux Rosebud Indian Reservation in South Dakota. The Los Angeles-based Catalina Island Conservancy had repatriated one hundred Little Buffalo to the Lakota, the "People of the Buffalo." The Catalina Island buffalo had been isolated on the island since 1927. The Native American film director Zane Grey had brought them from Yellowstone to be filmed in a movie entitled *Vanishing Americans*, one of the first films to tell of the Native Americans' struggle.

On the mainland, almost all other buffalo had been crossbred with cattle to create "beefalo" for beef production. The Catalina Island herd was one of the last remaining groups of true American Bison that had once numbered a hundred million.

On that frigid December morning, Leonard Crow Dog greeted the Little Buffalo as they arrived from Catalina Island, completing the cycle of the Sioux Ghost Dance. Leonard Crow

Dog was the great nephew of Jerome Crow Dog who years earlier had brought the Ghost Dance to the Sioux with Kicking Bear. Crow Dog was also the last Native American to be imprisoned for ghost dancing at the 1973 standoff at Wounded Knee. In 1978, four years after Leonard Crow Dog's imprisonment, Native Americans won back their right to free worship and the Ghost Dance was legal once again for the first time in eighty-eight years.

As Crow Dog welcomed the Little Buffalo home, he plucked a wad of white hair from one of the passing calves and gleefully shouted out, *"Tehenshila!"* recognizing them as the lost sacred herd. Crow Dog continued, "You will know the *Tehenshila* because they do a sacred thing, not because anyone says so."

In the spring of 2004, over one hundred of these repatriated buffalo seemed to disappear overnight from the Rosebud Indian Reservation. In response, the tribal chairman, Rodney Bordeaux, sent out a state alert to find the missing herd. When a police helicopter searched the Badlands the next day, they were amazed to see the Little Buffalo out beyond the limits of the reservation. The *Tehenshila* had rediscovered the long-lost remnants of the old migratory route of the extinct American Great Northern Herd: the Sioux's Hoop of Life.

Before there were Europeans or horses, millions of buffalo would make the yearly migration from the Black Hills to Yellowstone and back again. At specific sites along the way, the Sioux would perform the Seven Rites of the Sacred Pipe given to them by their female Messiah, White Buffalo Calf Woman. But the Hoop needed to be found before it could be mended and the Little Buffalo had led the way, signaling to the Ghost Dancer that the time to tie the final knot had arrived.

CHAPTER 26
THE SCRIBE

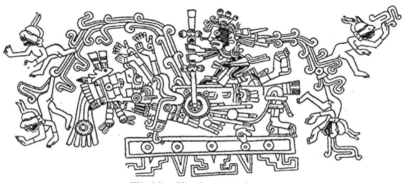

The New Fire Lighting Ceremony

F reed by the Toltec Ghost Dancer, *Tloloc Sequah* returned to his cave to help his friend, but he had arrived too late and the damage was done. While the rain god had been gone, the sacred cloud forest dried up, the Little Ones died and *Desheto*, the Prince of Plants, was gone. For the first time in history, *Desheto*, the voice of the Fruit of Knowledge had gone extinct. Though the rain god *Tloloc Sequah* whimpered at his loss, he still could not cry.

Gazing into the Pool of Origins, the Lord of Days saw the now-impotent rain god hiding in his cave. Without the rain, the Fruit of Knowledge had died, the Tree of Life was also dying and *Tezcatlipoca* could see that the Americas had reached a tipping point. As *Desheto* had once predicted, before the Ghost Dance ended, the mountains of ice would melt as the fertile plains of North America dried up into a dust bowl and the Great Jungle of the South burned. Knowing the destruction had already gone too far made even the Lord of Days shiver.

Unfortunately, humans had only obtained enough knowledge to destroy the Mother, but not the wisdom needed to properly care for her. Heartbroken by this human betrayal and the death of her beloved Prince *Desheto*, the Earth Mother decided she had no choice but to fight for her own life. She knew that if she didn't fight, the drought the humans had created would suck her as dry as it had the rain god.

MY TALE TO TELL

In Mexico's southern state of Oaxaca, the rainy season had always begun during May, but it was already the middle of June, 2007, and the rains had still not come. Over the past five decades, I, *Desheto*'s scribe Ani, had followed the Rope of the Dead, from my meetings with *Desheto* at Rancho Catalunya, Mexico, to the Amazon Jungle and then back up north to the place of the Ghost Dance's demise at Wounded Knee. It had been my greatest joy to know the last of the wild and free and also my greatest sorrow to witness their sad end.

Following the Rope of the Dead across the three continents of the Americas, I had found six of the seven pieces of the *tiponi* that the Toltec had hidden among the tribes. These shards had kept the Ghost Dance alive among the tribes that possessed them. They had endured through the entire cycle of the calendar and had led me to the Tree of Life and back again to the Mountains of the Clouds where it had all started.

The road ended at a backwater pueblo in Mexico's southern state of Oaxaca and the town had changed little in the eighteen years I'd been away following the rope. Standing in the plaza, I was consumed by a feeling of déjà vu as I turned towards the mountain peak where the ruins of the Sky Temple lay in rubble.

On the other side of the mountain, past *Chato's* cave, was the path that led to the sacred ground upon which *Quetzalcoatl* had first ghost danced and to Rancho Catalunya where this story began.

To my dismay, when I talked to the locals I met on the path, they told me that the hacienda at Rancho Catalunya had been mysteriously burned down. Then they joyfully assured me that since there was no more rain, a road would finally be built through their cloud forest and would bring in badly needed revenue. All I could think about was how *Desheto* would survive without the rain, but all these poor people could think about was how the road would somehow make them feel connected. Connected to what, I thought, the modern world which was quickly leaving them behind?

After eighteen years of drought, the mountains had dried up and no longer resembled their past grandeur. For hours I walked through the now-decrepit cloud forest searching through the glorious memories of my past. I struggled to come to terms with the fact that I was a dead man now walking through a forgotten dream. Death the Hunter had picked up my scent, and on instinct, like a wild animal, I headed for the bush of my awakening in order to await death, but without the rain the bush had disappeared.

Alongside the path, seated upon a large rock, as if he had been waiting for me, was my dear old friend Daniel. His hair had turned snow-white during the years I'd been away and he greeted me deadpan, as if I'd only been gone a month. "*De tin da-li, Maguey*, where have you been?"

We touched the tips of the fingers of our right hands and I answered with a bittersweet smile. "*Dali, shumbah*, trying to find my way back here."

After spending a lifetime following the rope, this was the closest place to a home I had ever known, but Daniel snickered, "Eighteen *pinche* years! You've gotten to be as slow as an old turtle." Then he stood up with his machete in his hand and took one of my bags with the other. It only took a few more steps for me to ask the question he was waiting for. "Have you seen him?"

Daniel shook his head before he replied. "No, he's gone. No one has seen the Little Ones or heard of *Desheto* since the hailstorm eighteen years ago when the Old Turtle died and the drought began. The people say that they've gone to "Gringolandia" and now *Desheto* only speaks English. Is that true?"

"I don't know," I answered. "I haven't spoken with him since I was last here."

We arrived at the village, a few shacks on a sun-dried hill that had once been nestled in moist clouds. We went inside Daniel's home where his wife Lucía was making tortillas.

Lucía greeted me with a warm hug and said, "Did Daniel tell you that he is gone?"

As I nodded yes, Lucía noticed my downhearted expression and said, "Don't be sad, *Maguey*. Catalunya is gone but things are better now. We have a church, a women's rights group, and the road will be here soon. It will bring money. We really need money."

Funny, I had always looked at the Clean Sisterhood as an ancient type of women's empowerment group, and it had seemed to me that the old-time religion was more effective than the church. I realized that maybe the changes were better for them, but not for me. The most profound thing I had ever experienced in a lifetime of experiencing many extraordinary things now seemed to be gone forever.

"*Desheto*'s gone, but we're still here, *Maguey*," Lucía reminded me. "Didn't you come to see us, too? Besides, I have the rancho-style *nock ma, nock may, ninyo*, beans and corn tortillas that you love."

Lucía was right and I smiled back. It felt good to lay eyes on them all once again and I did love her cooking. So I filled my belly with the flavor of the rancho, and boy, did it bring back memories. After dinner and just before darkness fell, I walked up the mountain towards *Chicón Nindo's* cave and strung a hammock in an old, empty shack along the path.

After brushing my teeth, I grabbed a book out of my pack, turned on my battery-powered lantern and rested in the hammock. My scholarly friend, Jim Walton, had given me a copy of the *Codex Borgia*, one of the very few Mesoamerican holy books that had survived the fires of the Inquisition. The book the *Codex Borgia* was originally copied from was written by Precious Flower's scribes in the same Sky Temple that now lay in ruin beyond the pueblo.

Although I had looked at these pictures many times, just being on *Chicón Nindo's* mountain made the images take on a new meaning. At its core, the *Codex* told the story of the Toltec Ghost Dancer's journey through the underworld. In splendid pictographs I could see him following the Rope of the Dead through the different ordeals and awakenings in the Black Flower. By following the Rope of the Dead, the Toltec Ghost Dancer went through the same divine transformation as his patron god, the Plumed Serpent.

One pictograph in particular caught my eye that night. It was an image of a ritual in which the Plumed Serpent stood back to back with the ghost of the Lord of the Dead. As I looked closer, I realized that the god and the ghost were not standing together, but rather were dancing, with their legs both raised up high. In that moment of clarity it came to me that I was looking at the earliest known depiction of the first ritual of the Americas: the Ghost Dance.

Here, below *Chicón Nindo's* cave, the image of the Ghost Dance had come alive, validated by the ancient scribes who had written the *Codex* to help future generations survive the Fifth World. I was excited by my discovery but quickly realized that it no longer mattered. Without *Desheto*, who had the knowledge needed to complete the ritual, the Ghost Dance would lose its power.

The main reason I had returned to the Mazateca was to finish *Desheto's* story of the Ghost Dance and fulfill my agreement as his scribe. I also had another agenda: to save the life of a friend and hopefully, by doing so, save my own. In the Mazatecan healing tradition, it is customary to never ask for anything for yourself but only to ask on behalf of another. So I came to ask for my fallen friend Jeremy who was dying of cancer. Jeremy had been a strong and healthy young warrior for Mother Nature but who, for no apparent reason, seemed to have been called upon by the Lady of the Dead.

As for my own illness, no one was really sure what was wrong. Some said it was chemical poisoning and others claimed that it was a Lakota spider witch's curse, but somehow a demon was running through my veins like liquid fire and eating me up alive. Neither top physicians nor the traditional healers I had consulted had a clue of how to help me. Even the great Lakota healer, Grandpa Roy Stone, who had cured many people, couldn't seem to make sense of my illness.

My last hope was *Desheto,* and I was hoping that after he saved Jeremy, *Desheto* would once again heal me as he had done twice before. But now it seemed that I had outlived *Desheto* and I had reached the end of the rope in my own Ninth Hell.

Through the dark of the night I tried to calm down by telling myself that it was too dangerous a time to indulge in fear, that I just didn't have that luxury. So I turned off the lantern and did what I had done so many times before: I lit a beeswax candle and focused on the crest of the candle's flame, whispering to the Lord of Fire and praying to him to bring his grandson warmth in a cold world.

As I gazed into the Grandfather's flame, I reminisced over the past forty years of my life, watching a chronological-order review of events play out in my mind like a lucid film. Every way I looked at it, the path always led back to the Old Turtle's death and the hailstorm. Those two events had ended my relationship with *Desheto* and something inside me had died.

Then the epidemics began in the Amazon and the hopelessness and suffering had made me hard and had stolen my dreams. I was left a vagabond upon the land, lost, confused and full of rage, tormented over the way a few had gotten rich raping the Earth Mother. I had lost all hope until I returned to the fields of the lord where I saw the *hekura* and *xapori* ghost dancing, ready to defend the Tree of Life.

Getting up out of the hammock, the song I had not sung and the dance I had not danced in eighteen years came back to me. As I danced for the ancestors, the Toltec Ghost Dancer whispered to me, saying that the seventh and final piece of the *tiponi,* which had not yet been found, had been hidden here all along. So, I sang to the rain god, for without rain, there is no hope. *"Tloloc Sequah, ah ey oh."*

I sang and sang until there was no strength left in me, but no rain came, so I sat in silence, opening myself up to the gods instead of trying to force my will. Taking a deep breath, I let my feelings flow and for a moment my thoughts became suspended in time. In the void of that moment I heard the pulse of my heartbeat turn into a gentle tapping on the roof and I could see *Tloloc Sequah*, the rain god, swelling up with emotions.

With humility and the deepest respect, I called out *Tloloc Sequah's* name one more time and then heard the forest go silent. A moment later, the god answered with a spectacular lightning bolt that flashed like a serpent's tongue and licked the dank underbellies of dark clouds, igniting the Crucible of the Summer Storm. Then, a deafening thunder exploded in the night, sending a deep rumble through the mountains, a rumble so profound it could only have been made by a god.

After the thunder, not an animal peeped nor a frog croaked, and the forest was still. Then the pitter-patter of raindrops broke the silence, as the rain god began to mourn the loss of his friend *Desheto*. Once he began to cry, the rain god could not control himself and the drizzle turned into a shower that was followed by a torrential downpour.

Eighteen years later, the drought had ended. I heard conch shells being blown by the people of the village and from the open door of my shack I could see candles being lit all across the dark mountain, shining like the stars of the night sky.

By early morning, after hours of downpour, the rain tapered into a drizzle. It was still not light out, so I pushed the button on my flashlight as I left the shack and walked down the path. Through the mist, I could see that the terrible rumble I had heard had been the sound of a large section of *Chicón Nindo's* mountain that had come down in a landslide, blocking the only pathway into his domain. The old gods were still alive.

Disheveled, drunk and soaked to the bone, my old friend Tío Julio stumbled out of the rubble in a cloud of mist and dust. This raggedy man had never once left the Little Ones' forest that was vanishing around him, nor learned to speak Spanish. Mazatecan was his only language. Tío Julio had paid the price for his resistance, and the loss had broken him with firewater. Julio saw me and could not believe his eyes, thinking that I was a ghost. He staggered to keep his balance, pointing towards the creek with one hand and pressed his forefinger tightly against his lips. Julio's bloodshot eyes opened wide and he whispered, "*Tío Maguey*, the Little Ones are back."

I stood dumbfounded as my heart soared with the possibility that *Desheto* was still alive. Only when Julio officially greeted me by touching the tips of his fingers to mine were we both convinced this was not a dream and I was not a ghost. Without another thought, we walked together down the slippery hillside and entered the sacred forest where Julio had lived all his life and the Little Ones had lived for thousands.

Along the creek, I caught the scent and bent down to gently clear away the underbrush. For the first time in eighteen years I saw the Little Ones. With great reverence, I apologized for cutting their lives short and then I placed the mushrooms in a large folded leaf. As I searched deeper, one by one, and then in families of four and five, the Little Ones appeared, springing forth from nowhere. I spent the morning gathering them.

For the villagers, the return of the Little Ones was more confusing. Over the last eighteen years they had lost the sacrament they had worshipped for thousands of years and with its loss, the Old Way seemed to have disappeared. But now, defying all logic, that old-time religion was raising its feathered head once again.

CHAPTER 27
DESHETO

Desheto, the Prince of Plants

Two gods faced each other at the end of the calendar cycle, their heads emerging from the dual mouths of the double-headed Vision Serpent that formed a ring around the Ghost Dancer's destiny. The Toltec Ghost Dancer had survived the underworld, danced with the ghosts, sung with the gods, talked with plants and learned what it was to carry the wild and free

Spirit of the Americas within him. Now it was time to tie the final knot and restore communication between the living and the dead.

Meticulously, the Toltec Ghost Dancer finished mending every last fiber of the rope except one. When he was nearly done, *Quetzalcoatl* and *Tezcatlipoca* cut the final dangling strand with which to tie his hands together and placed the rest of the fibers around his neck to make a leash. The Ghost Dancer submitted to the gods who led him to the serpent-headed Earth Mother's altar in the last of the twenty-two petals of the flower. The Toltec had finished his grail journey and completed his task. Now it was time for his ghost to die so his spirit could cross back over into the realm of the living and dance with a human partner again.

When the two gods had laid the Toltec Ghost Dancer across the Earth Mother's altar, *Quetzalcoatl* said, "Life is the awakening from death's dream which can only be remembered by dying again."

Quetzalcoatl then held the Toltec Ghost Dancer's arms and *Tezcatlipoca* held his bony legs, as the Earth Mother plunged an obsidian knife into his skeletal ribcage. The Toltec ghost gasped but did not scream, and as his bones settled, the eternal flame on the shore of the Pool of Origins was extinguished. Then there was only darkness in the Black Flower.

THE RITUAL

In the tiny shack below *Chicón Nindo's* cave, I fasted in preparation for my meeting with *Desheto* and spent all day working on the story of the Ghost Dance. Over the course of three decades, *Desheto* had told me a different part of the story each time I met with him, which I wrote down in the order of our meetings. *Desheto's* episodes did not follow a linear timeline because he did not seem to differentiate between the past, present and future, making it difficult to understand the plot of the story.

But after the Old Turtle had died, I began to arrange the episodes in the correct order, and over time the meaning of the story began to emerge. The Ghost Dance, based on the ancient Prophecy of Seven Generations, followed the journey of the Toltec Ghost Dancer as he saved the Tree of Life by following the Rope of the Dead to its source, the Fruit of Knowledge. The chapters of the book coincided with the thirteen awakenings and nine ordeals of the Black Flower that the Ghost Dancer had to go through in order to fulfill the prophecy. Only then could the Ghost Dancer save the Tree of Life and be transformed into the Plumed Serpent, the wild and free Spirit of the Americas.

When the sun went down and the clouds rolled in, I put my journal away. As I began to prepare for the night ahead, I heard the droning sound of a conch shell trumpet being blown in the distance, signaling the arrival of an incoming storm. A moment later, my old friend Papa Beto and his family appeared from the mist with wildflowers, a beeswax candle and copal incense for my altar. After they departed, it began to drizzle and I waited alone for the right time to begin my ritual: the moment just after dusk, between day and night.

As darkness fell, I closed the door and ignited the copal incense with a burning piece of charcoal. Then I lit the candle and gazing into the crest of its flame, I humbly petitioned the aid of the oldest god: Grandfather Fire.

"Grandfather Fire, *Huehueteotl*, it is I, *Desheto*'s scribe, *Ani*. You through whom all the gods must speak, I come to you first and ask your blessing, Grandfather, to call upon *Desheto*, the Prince of Plants."

Then the frogs began to sing and I knew that Grandfather Fire had heard me, so I opened the large folded leaf, took out the

Little Ones and passed them through the copal smoke to purify their souls. I ate the Little Ones in pairs so their journey to the Flower of the Dead would not be lonely. The mushrooms were acrid but edible and I relished every bite, fearing that these might be the very last of the Fruit of Knowledge ever to grow.

When I finished, I whispered, "*Nina ski-tah chili*; the gods give to those who give to the gods."

In the Mazatec tradition only *naguali* witches may ask for something from the gods or spirits for themselves. Healers and all others must make a request for someone else, so I asked for help for my friend Jeremy, a young warrior for the Earth Mother who was now extremely ill. After finishing my prayer, I put out the candle with the belled top of a flower and lay down on a straw mat in the darkness.

Lying on the floor, I could hear raindrops falling one by one and the cold began to seep in. When a chill came over me, I wrapped myself in a blanket until the cold gradually turned into colored waves of soothing warmth. Then that warmth grew fur and it seemed that all the fuzzy animals of the forest were cuddling with me on the floor. Their tender caresses quieted my thoughts and I could hear the Little Ones in my stomach begin to chatter with rising expectations. The sacred mushrooms wanted to tell the story of their lives before they were digested and gone forever.

"We have been waiting, but we are not from here. We've come from a star far away. Now He's coming. We always knew you were the right choice."

Was I really? All I knew for sure was that I had once again let an outside entity into my body. Huh! I laughed at myself, a middle-aged man being possessed by a talking mushroom, alone in the most notoriously dangerous bandito-ridden backwoods of Mexico.

With this growing awareness of my own vulnerability, a nervous tension began to build and the Little Ones started to die in my stomach. I struggled to maintain composure against the rising surge of energy until an ecstatic rush exploded my world into a thousand tiny pieces. The blast knocked me unconscious, only to be awakened into another reality. I now perceived the world through the network of plants.

The forest was no longer background scenery; instead, now the plants and trees had all become green conspirators, ready to defend the Tree of Life. As I listened, I could hear the plants whispering secrets to each other under the cover of night. At first, I wasn't sure if it was just my own desire, or if those whispers had actually begun to blend into the faint melody I most yearned to hear: *Desheto*'s song. I hadn't heard his song in so long I had begun to wonder if it had ever existed anywhere other than in my head. But now there it was, the sound of the cloud forest slowing down into a bubbling underwater melody.

Hidden by the rain, like a thief in the night, the Prince of Plants left the sacred cloud forest and followed the path of his song to the entrance of my shack.

As the door blew open announcing *Desheto*'s arrival, a flurry of iridescent Wind Serpents burst in, filling the darkness with a brilliant mosaic of colorful illumination. Hidden by the dancing mosaic of light, a rain-soaked presence slipped into the shadows in the corner of the hut. Like any wild creature cornered within four walls, *Desheto* was not comfortable in an enclosed space. But as his breathing calmed, my shy guest began to whisper in an archaic tongue that had taken me decades to truly understand.

"I am a speck of dust blown across the universe, a vagabond upon the wind. *Dali, Ani*, I am the Prince of Plants and it is good to see you again, my scribe."

"*Dali de tin de,* my Prince, is that really you?" I questioned. "Everyone said that you were dead."

Desheto answered, "It is true, I did die, but then I returned from the Black Flower where the Grateful Dead now sing for the ghost of Jeremy. The dead have already sent the hummingbirds and Jeremy will soon hear the song of their wings. I grieve for those who will suffer from his loss, but he has been blessed by the Mother and will become a ghost who dances with the living. In this way, Jeremy will fulfill his dream to help heal the tattered relationship between the children and their Mother. Ghost Dancers need dancing ghosts as partners and Jeremy will become a Hummingbird Warrior, the greatest honor the Mother gives to a son."

For a long moment, I lay there in silence trying to come to terms with Jeremy's imminent passing. I felt as if I had abandoned my friend to die, but then the smell of ammonia and roses suddenly brought me back to my senses. The scent of Death the Hunter reminded me that I too was being stalked. As my survival instincts took over, I bargained with *Desheto* for my life.

"*Desheto*," I confided, "I realize that my destiny is in your hands and if today is a good day to die, then that's the way it will be. But how will I complete our agreement and finish the story of the Ghost Dance if my time has come?"

When the Prince of Plants didn't answer, I questioned my sanity and wondered if perhaps the ethnobiologist Richard Evan Schultes had been right: I had ventured so far into the world of plants that I could never completely come back to what we call reality.

Desheto finally spoke. "That's why I chose you to be my scribe. Who else would be crazy enough to spend his life following a rope that cannot be seen? And look at you tonight, completely vulnerable, surrounded by danger and talking to a voice no one else can hear. It has only been your faith in me that has kept you going on the path of the Rope of the Dead."

Fear gave way to a dark humor and I laughed with the rain in that desolate shack, knowing *Desheto* was right. Sure, I had stumbled along the way, but I had never let go of the Rope of the Dead. Following the path of the rope had led me to six of the seven tribes of the Americas among whom the Toltec Ghost Dancer had hidden the sacred shards of the *tiponi*. The ancestors of these tribes had danced with me and, together, we returned the memory of the Ghost Dance to the living tribes. Only after I had danced with the ancestral ghosts and seen the Tree of Life did the Rope of the Dead lead me back to the source, to *Desheto*, to find the seventh shard and finish a story that had taken him more than half my lifetime to tell.

Deep in thought, I didn't notice the rain had stopped and as the sky cleared, the scent of Death the Hunter had passed. Looking through the open shack doorway, I saw candlelight shining out through the cracks in the boards of Lucía's kitchen below my mountaintop perch. Lucía, a Clean Sister, had been sitting in vigil in front of a small altar while Daniel rested in the corner, wrapped in a blanket. Lucía prayed to the goddess *Tonantzin* in her guise as the Virgin Mother, Our Lady of Guadalupe, asking for her to oversee my journey and protect me from harm.

Looking past Lucía's candlelight, I was drawn outside by the most unusual night sky I had ever seen. There were so many stars covering the heavens, they appeared to have merged together to form a white veil, but I soon recognized that this blanket of stars was just part of the Lord of Witches' illusion. The stars I saw weren't really there but, instead, had burnt out a long time ago.

What remained was the light left behind in the gap of time it took for that light to travel far enough for me to see it.

"Now, look away from this starry illusion and place your ear to the ground to listen," *Desheto* directed me.

I bent down and put my ear to the damp ground, and as I listened, a faint and distant rumble seemed to rise up from the bowels of the earth, getting louder as it approached. When the rumble grew into the unbearable roar of a stampede, *Desheto* told me to look up. A moment later, with a thunderous crash, the *hekura*, or animal spirits of the Little Buffalo, tore through *Tezcatlipoca's* starry Veil of Illusion and appeared as shooting stars, falling from a black tear in the texture of the sky just below the Milky Way. The *hekura* of the Little Buffalo that White Buffalo Calf Woman had released from the Black Flower had done the unimaginable; they had ripped a hole in *Tezcatlipoca's* Veil of Illusion. That day, in homage to the Little Buffalo, a giant solar flare that formed the shape of a flaming buffalo on the sun's surface was observed by astronomers.

Overwhelmed by the synchronicity of the moment, I was barely able to crawl back inside the shack and close the door. Once inside, I calmed myself down and relit the candle of Grandfather Fire's flame. As I sat in front of that sacred fire once again, I heard *Desheto's* words paint panoramas that evolved and changed as he spoke.

"Now that the illusion is torn, look and see the future."

Terrifying visions of plagues, a blood-red ocean, melting glaciers, parched deserts and burning forests passed through my troubled mind. At the center of my vision were the *hekura* and *xapori* huddled around the Tree of Life at El Dorado.

Like *kachinas* from another world, the spirits crouched in a constant vigil, knowing the would-be assassins of the Mother were circling for the kill. They wore suits with ties instead of knives, poised to remove anyone who got in the way of their mother lode, even if it meant killing the Tree of Life.

Desheto was emphatic. "Witches have infected the rapists of Mother Nature with demons of greed and now their hunger has become rabid and cannot be fulfilled. Only the Ghost Dance can stop them, but somewhere along the way the people have lost the steps to the dance and that is why I commissioned you to be my scribe, *Ani*, to retrieve those steps."

I tried to comprehend the magnitude of what *Desheto* was saying, but my thoughts were racing, changing directions as quickly as I could think them. I searched the annals of my mind, hoping to come across an artifact I had overlooked in my quest to find an answer, but instead I kept coming back to the death of the Old Turtle. After his death, something in me had also died and I had become consumed by the illusion and started to yearn for the white man's treasure. I was not immune to the greed and arrogance that the illusion created. I had become one of *Pahana*'s wayward children, but then the Rope of the Dead led me back to the Tree of Life.

Desheto quickly dismissed my momentary pride that had come from my realization that I had finally returned to the Rope of the Dead. He foretold the quickly approaching fulfillment of the Prophecy of Seven Generations that he had begun to tell me almost five decades earlier. In that moment, I realized that my own dance with the ghosts was coming full circle.

Desheto spoke. "Soon they will come out of the forest, the people and animals that were believed to no longer exist. The last of the wild and free are emerging because they can sense that the forest, their world, is dying and so is yours."

Overwhelmed by his words, my mind began to race, looking for some way out of this, but Desheto cut back in to continue his prophecy before I could regain my balance.

"Soon, the long lost Children of the Wild and Free will stand up and face those who believe it is their right to consume the Mother without any respect. At this time when the Protectors face the Destroyers and Tezcatlipoca's veil can no longer cover the truth with illusion, the final cycle of this Ghost Dance will manifest in the world of the living. Then, the *hekura* and the *xapori*, the most sacred of the ancestral ghosts, will dance back into the world of the living.

When Desheto finished speaking, my mind returned to the vision. I could see below the canopy of the Amazon Jungle, where the rapists of the forest were now quickly approaching. At the same time the *xapori* and *hekura* called upon the thorny and poisonous plants to form a barrier around the Tree of Life. The most venomous serpents and fierce predators of the jungle had come to guard the barrier, along with tiny insects that carried the Plague Mother's infinitesimal white worms.

When all the creatures of the jungle had finally gathered together to defend the tree, the wild and free Spirit of the Americas let out a mighty roar. Having waited for this moment since he left his mountain home, the Plumed Serpent came crashing out of the bush, riding upon the crest of a tempestuous wind. In a thunderstorm of lightning, wind and rain, the plumed apparition circled the Tree of Life, whirling around the jungle floor like a bee-stung dervish. The feathered beast was hungry to feed upon the souls of the two-legged murderers of Mother Nature.

Watching the drama unfold, I felt embarrassed and guilty for the atrocities humans had inflicted on Mother Nature. Troubled by these thoughts, I questioned *Desheto*. "Why do plants care if people live or die when we have made so much trouble for the earth and her creatures?"

Desheto exhaled deeply and answered. "Because you are part of us, the other side that makes us whole. During the day you breathe the air the plants provide you, but it is your night breath of dreams, the air you breathe out when you sleep, that is sweeter than any other for plants. Plants will help humans for the sweet breath of their dreams alone because for us it is ambrosia."

"Let me get this straight. Plants are going to save us because they like our breath and you have made me your scribe so you could secure a steady supply of this ambrosia?" I quipped, befuddled by his response.

Desheto replied, "As my blood gives you visions, your ambrosia also gives plants visions. I made you my scribe so humans can never say the plants have not warned them, not because I'm hoarding your tortilla breath, *pendejo*."

Desheto had had enough small talk by then and began to chant, rocking back and forth until the shadows quivered in the darkness. He had explained everything he could and now it was time to take action and fulfill his own Prophecy of Seven Generations. As I realized that this was *Desheto*'s ceremony not mine, the forest went completely silent and the Prince of Plants began his incantation.

"I call upon the Kingdom of Plants to claim the pieces of the *tiponi* as one and take back authority over the land. I am not a lily that is born and dies in the spring; I am *Desheto*, the Prince of Plants."

Although *Desheto* was in Mexico and the Tree of Life was rooted in the Amazon Jungle, the two could communicate through the mycelia that reached across the Americas. Answering the Prince of Plants' incantation, the subterranean mycelia of the Tree of Life reached out through a creeping network of fungus to communicate with every plant and tree in the Americas. This network of mycelia is the brain behind that which controls the weather, the very thing civilization needs to survive. The Prince of Plants was not begging humans to respect the Mother. Instead, using the Tree of Life's mycelia, he had turned the entire Kingdom of Plants against the horrors of the human destruction of nature.

Desheto whispered, "Let them know we are waiting, scribe, so they can never say they have not been warned."

Then *Desheto* unexpectedly leapt out from the shadows and I retreated, afraid he was going to take out his anger towards humans on me. We danced, back and forth, anticipating each other's moves, constantly on guard from attack. While we danced, *Desheto* called upon the wind to orchestrate the movement of the trees and they began to sway in unison as they tossed about the leafy manes of their canopy. Dancing together like a freestyle chorus line, they began to affect the weather, causing heavy, black clouds to return.

"The Two-Legged Ones think plants are helpless and at their mercy but they are wrong; humans are at our mercy. I called upon the Mother of All Plagues to cull the human herd."

In a ritualistic attack Desheto circled, forcing me to join him in a dance for my life.

Each time his shadow passed by me, I held my ground, anticipating his next move in the hope of curbing his instinct to strike. "*Tezcatlipoca* was wrong. The gods never needed to destroy the Two-legged Ones, for they will destroy themselves," the Prince of Plants baited me.

His constant barrage wore me out and *Desheto* finally took me down, whispering in my ear.

"You have also been infected with the illusion and so you cannot finish this story until you have been purged. Now, let go and the Little Ones will take civilization's poison out of you."

A dark-gray dust vibrated and buzzed, growing inside me, overtaking me with every breath. There was no pain, just the smell of ammonia and roses along with a tingling warmth. As awareness of myself slipped away, I was calm but still dying. In my mind's eye, I saw a little person bathed in light at the beginning of a long, blue road. She had a bowl haircut and she smiled as butterflies, hummingbirds and bees flew around her. The gray dust was repelled by her smile, a smile filled with life force. Her smile transformed the butterflies, hummingbirds and bees into ancestral ghosts.

Chanting in the ancient way and dancing in a choreographed line, two of the ancestors lifted my tired spirit. On my right was the Old Turtle and on my left was the Toltec Ghost Dancer. Carrying my soul, they danced counterclockwise from west to east and I recorded every detail and step in my mind, hoping to remember the steps back from the world of the dead.

I awoke to the singing of the Clean Sisters and began to dance like a possessed puppet on a string. The Old Turtle and Toltec Ghost Dancer watched from the side, their eyes reflecting faith in what I was doing. As I danced back to back with the ghost of the Lord of the Dead, I felt the Little Ones in my stomach begin their own death dance. They bubbled and gurgled to the sound of an underwater marimba and I began to gag.

Suddenly, the Little Ones leapt out of my stomach, emerging as a vomit of black mud that spewed out six feet across the shack's interior. When the retching stopped, *Desheto* continued. "For the next seven days, bathe in my forest's waters where the plant called the Goat Herder's Daughter grows, and you will be cured. Then maybe, my doubting scribe, you will believe in yourself enough to finish what you have started."

The Prince of Plants vanished into the night before the Morning Star appeared in the sky and I began to gather the shattered pieces of my reality together. Simple tasks like cleaning brought me back down to earth and I realized that one of my favorite parts of ghost dancing with *Desheto* was simply the high of having survived the occasion.

Over the next seven days, as *Desheto* had instructed me, I bathed in the creek beside the plants of the Goat Herder's Daughter.

On the first day after the ceremony, I was full of hope and it was hard to define the line between my vision and reality as I still felt the euphoria of the Little Ones' blood within me. Since I had had little education, learning to write had proved to be one of the most difficult parts of the journey, so if nothing else, I had kept my word and become his scribe.

On the second day, I maintained my hope, but the Little Ones' blood within me was fading fast and cracks started to form in my conviction.

On the third day after bathing, I wrestled with demons, attempting to stop my heart from falling back into the hopelessness of victimhood. I questioned my benefactor's motives, wondering whether he had a personal agenda for making me his scribe. Could it be that *Desheto* had taken forty-five years of my life to groom me to write a defense for his own survival? I came to an uneasy peace, deciding to suspend doubt for awhile longer.

On the fourth day, I saw the blue, red, orange and yellow offspring of the Plumed Serpent race across the grass and I took it as a sign. The snake had the same markings as the Plumed Serpent and just seeing it reopened my mind to possibilities. I wanted to believe there was a way out of the mess that humanity had gotten itself into.

On the fifth day of bathing, I felt I was beginning to awaken from a very long dream in which time was catching up with me.

All the seemingly unrelated ordeals and revelations I had survived following the Rope of the Dead were starting to come together. For the first time I realized that, although many tribes had different styles of ghost dancing, the purpose was always the same: to commune with the ancestral ghosts who knew the correct way to live. The Ghost Dance was a ritual of learning that could teach people to see through the illusion and commune with the forces of nature. By coming to terms with the gods, we could save our niche in the weave of nature.

On the sixth day, the ritual took on a deeper meaning with the awareness that the Ghost Dance existed on four different levels at the same time, in the underworld, the world of the living, the microscopic and the cosmic levels simultaneously. While Venus played out the ritual in the sky, the gods ghost danced as did the ghosts of the ancestors and humans, too. How could I have ever known that all these facets of the ritual existed without following its steps and how could I have understood *Desheto*'s meaning without following the Rope of the Dead to the edge of the world and seeing the Tree of Life?

I awoke on the seventh morning hopeful that *Desheto*'s healing had worked, but when I looked at my skin it seemed worse than ever, oozing with an infected rash. Doubt overcame me in a wave of fear and my stomach tied itself into a knot. After all this, I was still rotting and dying. It seemed I had been forsaken by the gods, or at least by myself. Nevertheless, I pulled myself together and bathed in the waters as instructed.

The next night, the eighth, I had tortured dreams of the Toltec Ghost Dancer sprawled out across Mother Nature's snake altar with his heart cut out. *Quetzalcoatl* and *Tezcatlipoca* had made a fire in his empty chest cavity with a fire-starting hand drill. The fire of a new calendar cycle was lit and the smoke that rose from the Toltec Ghost Dancer's chest cavity carried his soul back into the world of the living.

On the ninth morning, I woke up scratching and unknowingly peeled an entire layer of skin off the side of my face. In a state of panic, I grabbed my bloodstained sheet and ran down to the creek of the Goat Herder's Daughter. The creek was in a mysterious part of the sacred cloud forest that was covered with a square-stemmed plant. This plant, *Salvia Divinorum*, also known as Sage of the Diviners and Seer's Sage, was the sacred plant of the Olmec that the human *Quetzalcoatl* had eaten with Precious Flower in the time before the Little Ones had arrived in the Mazateca.

Puzzled, I stood on the rocks at the edge of the watering hole looking down at a man floating under a sheet, submerged face down in the water. I wanted to leap in and save him but I couldn't. I was spellbound and drowning in my own fears. Then, instinct took over and I jumped into the pool. Gasping for air, I came up out of the water with only the sheet in my hands.

Choking, I crawled up onto the rocks, touching myself to make sure I was still alive. With each touch, my skin came loose and slowly I shimmied out of three huge pieces of peeled flesh, like a snake shedding its skin. Just as *Desheto* had predicted, when the diseased skin was removed there was healthy skin underneath and I realized that I had been cured.

Each year since then, when the rains come, I have returned to the Mountains of the Clouds. With the revival of the Little Ones, the old-time religion has returned, and once again *Desheto* speaks to me about the nature of life. He talks about the relationship between the Mother, plants, animals, stars, people, ghosts and gods but has never again spoken of the Ghost Dance.

Throughout these years I have worked on recording these events, watching the world as it has raced towards a perilous future and the tipping point that *Desheto* predicted. Hopefully, I have finished my job as *Desheto*'s scribe before it is too late and before his words have lost their meaning.

I am *Ani*, scribe to *Desheto*, the Prince of Plants, and I have written his story of the Ghost Dance so Americans can find their grail and rise up like plumed serpents. This calendar cycle has been completed, the eternal Flame has been relit and the Ghost Dance begins anew.

Nina ski-tah chili. The gods give to those that give to the gods.

So let's dance.

Photo Gallery

Michael Stuart Ani taking part in an epene psychotropic snuff ritual with Yanomami tribesmen of the Amazon (Photo by Arnold Newman)

Michael Stuart Ani taking part in a epene ritual with José Valero, the son of the Yanomami Chief Fusiwe and the kidnapped Brazilian, Helena Valero (Photo by Leslie Baer Dinkle)

The Little Ones (Photo by Heather Vuchinich)

Finding the Little Ones (Photo by Heather Vuchinich)

Glossary and List of Characters

Amautas

An Ayumara medicine man. Bolivian President Evo Morales is of the Ayumara tribe.

Awanyu

The horned version of the Plumed Serpent god within the Hopi tradition who represents the phallic power of the universe.

Aya Marcay Quilla or "Mouth Wide Open"

The Aya Marcay Quilla is the Peruvian version of the Ghost Dance and involves the ghost of the ancestor emerging from the mouth of the Vision Serpent.

Centeotl

The Aztec god of corn who was associated with the group of stars known as the Pleiades. This constellation marks the entrance to the Vision Serpent's throat. Centeotl was first a goddess and the daughter of the earth goddess, but then later became a god, representing both the feminine and masculine elements of corn.

CHALCIHUITLICUE

The Aztec goddess of fresh waters, especially rivers and streams. Chalcihuitlicue is also the goddess of childbirth and her body is a portal for the manifestation of ghosts.

CHATO

The Mazatecan god of lust who came after the arrival of the Europeans and became the gatekeeper to the sacred world of Desheto. He guards the path to the sacred mountain of Chicón Nindo from his cave in a river gorge below the Puente de Fierro beside a tiny village in the Mazateca of Oaxaca, Mexico.

CHICÓN NINDO

Lord of the Mountain overlooking the home of the Little Ones. Chicón Nindo is the Mazatecan version of the Plumed Serpent and from his semen the Little Ones are born.

CHICÓN TOKOSHO

Lord of the Mountain overlooking the hamlet of Huautla de Jimenez, Oaxaca. (Huautla is the town that became world famous for its sacred mushrooms after an article about it was featured in *Life* magazine.) ChicónTokosho is a god of commerce who appears as a giant snake. He is a manifestation of the Aztec Lord of Witches, Tezcatlipoca.

CHUNUPA

The sacred pipe of the Sioux given to them by their female messiah: White Buffalo Calf Woman. The Chunupa has both male and female parts and is the sacred instrument used in the seven rites that make the Lakota 'true' human beings.

COATLICUE

The serpent-skirted Earth Mother who gave birth to the Aztec people. She was born through the death of the Great Earth Monster and blessed to become the Earth Mother or Mother Nature.

COMADRES LIMPIADAS OR "CLEAN SISTERS"

Members of an ancient sisterhood of healers committed to the cleanliness of body and spirit who were the first group of women to be burned as witches during the Inquisition in the New World. The Clean Sisters were entrusted with the preservation of Mother Earth by protecting the ritual of the Ghost Dance and ensuring the survival of the dance and its dancers.

COYOLXAUHQUI

A daughter of the gods who became a gatekeeper on the pathway to both the heavens and the underworld. She was murdered and dismembered and then born again as the Aztec moon goddess.

DESHETO

The Prince of Plants is the spirit who speaks through the Little Ones, which are the mushrooms known as the Fruit of Knowledge. Desheto arrived during the first Ghost Dance and, through him, the Little Ones became the first plant to learn how to communicate with humans.

EHECATL

The Plumed Serpent manifesting as the Lord of the Wind. The Lord of the Wind is one of the Plumed Serpent's four faces. Ehecatl is depicted as a man wearing a duck-billed mask. As the Plumed Serpent, he danced the first Ghost Dance with the Lord of the Dead.

EJIDOS

Plots of tribal community land shared by a village to help those whose crops have failed. The ancient ejido system was reintroduced during the colonial era by the Catholic priest Bartolomé de Las Casas to help the indigenous people of Mexico.

GRATEFUL DEAD

The ape-like giants who lived in the Americas before Native Americans. Their bones were fertilized by the Plumed Serpent at the first Ghost Dance to make the ancestors of human beings.

HEKURA

The Yanomami word for the spirit of an animal that hides in the shadows and has the power to enter the human body to give power or cause illness.

HUEHUETEOTL OR GRANDFATHER FIRE

The oldest of the gods who lives in the crest of a flame. The bearded Grandfather Fire acts as a mediator between humans and gods. Huehueteotl is the giver of warmth in times of cold and the alchemist who transforms food with fire. He heals with fire but can also burn those who do not respect his powers. Known as Tatewari in the Huichol tradition and Thunkashila for the Lakota.

HUICHOL OR "EATERS OF PEYOTE"

The Huichol are a tribe of central Mexico who were never conquered by the Aztec. The tribal sacrament of the Huichol is the peyote cactus.

HUITZILOPOCHTLI OR LEFT-SIDED HUMMINGBIRD

The sun god and god of war with a heart beating with the stamina of a hummingbird. He sent the Aztec to conquer Mexico and demanded human sacrifice.

INIPI OR SWEAT LODGE

The shape of the lodge represents the stomach of a buffalo. The Inipi ritual is one of the seven sacred rites of the Sioux given to them by their female messiah, White Buffalo Calf Woman. Inside the Inipi, water is poured on hot stones creating intense steam while participants chant and commune with ancestral spirits.

KACHINA

The Hopi spirits of ancient beings who live in the San Francisco Peaks of Arizona. Hopi gods sent them to teach the Hopi people the proper way to live in peace.

KAUYUMARI

A name for the sacred, blue deer of the Huichol. Peyote cactus are said to grow in the footsteps of the *Kauyumari*.

KEESH-SHE-LA-MIL-LANG OR THE MASTER OF LIFE

The supreme god force that is beyond male and female, animal or human. The spirit of creation that created all other gods.

KIVA

The sacred ant house used by the Hopi in their rituals. This house is an underground chamber where sacred rituals are performed and the Kachinas can communicate.

KON TIKI VIRACOCHA

The South American version of the human form of the Plumed Serpent/Stranger who came from across the sea. Kon Tiki Viracocha is also the creator of civilization.

LITTLE ONES

The sacred mushrooms of the Mazatec people. The Little Ones grow in one particular cloud forest of the Sierra Mazateca. They were born from the seed of the Plumed Serpent and are humankind's original Fruit of Knowledge.

MAGUEY

The plant from which mescal is produced and a bastardization of the name Miguel. It is the name used by the Mazatec for the scribe Ani, the narrator of the text of this book. They used it so that outsiders would not know whom they meant.

MAMAS
The holy men of the Kogi Indians. They still live in the Sierra Nevada of Colombia. The Mamas believe that they are the guardians of the elements of nature.

MARA-AKAME
A Huichol medicine man who has the ability to view the world through the eyes of plants.

MAZATEC
An ancient tribal group of Oaxaca, Mexico, who are also called The People of the Clouds. They are the human guardians of the Little Ones and Desheto.

MICCAILHUITONTLI
The time of the year that the Aztec Lady of the Dead ceremony took place. This was the season when the Little Ones, the mushrooms used as the sacrament of the ritual, grew. The ceremony was performed at the time of day when the Vision Serpent's mouth in the Milky Way was wide open. This ceremony is the origin of the modern Day of the Dead holiday.

MICTECACIHUATL
The Lady of the Dead and ruler of the underworld of Mictlán, a place the Aztec poets called The Black Flower. Mictecacihuatl

angered her husband, Mictlantecuhtli, by helping the young Lord of the Wind to find the bones of the Grateful Dead.

MICTECACIHUATLAN

The name of the pueblo where the Lady of the Dead Ghost Dance ceremony was first performed. It was later ransacked by the conquistador Cortés as he made his way to the Aztec capital.

MICTLANTECUHTLI

The skeletal ghost and Lord of the Dead who ruled with Mictecacihuatl the Black Flower underworld. He danced the first Ghost Dance with the Lord of the Wind. His spirit animal is an owl called Death the Hunter.

MIXTEC

A large ethnic group living in the mountains of Oaxaca, Mexico. The Mixtec were the most prized artisans of the Aztec and their traditions provide a direct lineage to the ancient past.

NAGUAL

A totem animal spirit who can be sent into the dreams of others. It also can help to lead a person's spirit through the world of the dead. A Nagual can be a patron spirit of a people and place, as the Plumed Serpent is the totem spirit of the Americas.

OLMEC

The name given to the first known culture of Mexico. Taken from the Aztec name for the elder god of creation: Ometecuhtli/Omecihuatl. The Olmec culture flourished in the present-day state of Veracruz at the bottom of the Mountains of the Clouds and merged with the Mixtec to become the Southern half of the Toltec culture.

OMAVE

The Yanomami god of culture, art, healing and change. Omave is a manifestation of the Plumed Serpent. Like Pahana, Omave also traveled to faraway lands and returned home with diseases.

PAHANA

The white brother, in the Hopi tradition, whose misbehaving children bring environmental destruction down upon the world. Pahana will someday return to help teach his children how to behave before they destroy the human niche within nature.

PERIPO-YOMA

The Daughter of the Moon who was killed with arrows, and through her death, the Yanomami were born.

PEYOTEROS

The name for the Huichol Indians who search out and consume buttons of the sacred peyote cactus. Each year they make the journey to collect peyote and seek the visions it brings.

PIQUETE-ZINA

The bat god who is the sacred messenger of the forest and carries the spirit of the wild and free. Through him, all the spirits of the forest communicate and plan their defense against the assassins of the Earth Mother. In the Toltec creation myth,

Piquete-zina bites the Lord of the Wind to draw the blood used to create humans at the first Ghost Dance.

POPOL VUH
One of the few remaining ancient Mayan holy books. It tells the story of the journey through the underworld and how humans learn to deal with the gods.

PRECIOUS FLOWER
The once-human goddess of growing plants, nubile beauty, sensuality and life force. She is the spirit of young love and was the lover of the Stranger who became the human form of the god Quetzalcoatl. Wirikuta is her name in the Huichol language, Xochiquetzal for the Aztec.

QUETZALCOATL OR THE PLUMED SERPENT
The patron god of the Toltec and a spiritual totem of the Americas. Quetzalcoatl is the symbol of the wind and the indomitable essence of the wild and free.

TEHENSHILA
The sacred herd of little buffalo from which the Lakota messiah, White Buffalo Calf Woman, first appeared out of a snowstorm with a small white buffalo.

TEONANACATL OR "ASTONISHING GIFT OF THE GODS"

The Aztec word for sacred mushrooms, which includes the Little Ones, used as a sacrament in rituals like the Ghost Dance.

TEPEYOLLOTL

The Mesoamerican god Jaguar Heart of the Mountain is one of the many manifestations of the Lord of Witches or Tezcatlipoca. Tepeyollotl represents the belief that mountains are alive with a heart and soul. His roar can cause earthquakes.

TEZCATLIPOCA

The Aztec Lord of Witches and also the Lord of Days, adapted from the Toltec. Tezcatlipoca helped create the fifth world after his foot was bitten off and consumed by the Earth Monster. He is the most powerful of all the Aztec gods.

THUNKASHILA

The Lakota name for the fire god, also known as Grandfather Fire. In Mazatec, he is called Huehueteotl and for the Huichol, he is Tatewari.

TIPONI OR SACRED CHILD

The Hopi word for a set of jaguar bone pieces which, once all possessed, gives authority over the land to the possessor. The tiponi bones have a carving on them of a map to the sacred Tree of Life.

TLALTECUHTLI
The Toltec Earth Monster who was transformed into Mother Nature by consuming the poisonous foot of her son, the Lord of Days, Tezcatlipoca.

TLAZOLTEOTL
The Aztec goddess of witches, menstrual blood and filth who flies around on a broom. She is also the goddess of lust and sex magic.

TLOLOC SEQUAH
The Mixtec/Mazatecan name for the god of rain. The gods of rain, earth, lightning and wind are all needed to allow the Little Ones to Grow. Tloloc Sequah is one of the main gods of their civilization.

TOLOACHE
The psychotropic plant Datura, also called jimsonweed, which causes powerful visions. It can be dangerously toxic.

TOLTEC OR "THOSE WHO CAN BUILD FROM NOTHING"
The Toltec were the ancient Mexican tribe from whom the Aztec adopted their culture. There are stories that their existence spanned over a thousand years of peace. They used the Little Ones at their ceremonial center at Teotihuacan.

TONANTZIN

The mother spirit from whom Our Lady of Guadalupe was created. She embodies the traits of purity and virtue and is similar to the Virgin Mary.

TONATIUH

The Aztec's hungry sun god who lusts for the effervescence exuded around a still-beating heart pulled from a sacrificial victim.

VELADA

A candle ceremony, in this case, as performed by Mazatecan healers and witches alike, using the Little Ones mushroom for its sacrament.

VISHALIKA

The ancient name of the Huichol Indians of Mexico who resisted and remained unconquered by the Aztec.

VISION SERPENT

Its fully open mouth provides a portal and means for ancestral ghosts to enter this realm or reality. The Celestial Vision Serpent is located at the center of the Milky Way with its mouth, a black hole.

WASHANI NAGAI

The Shahaptian Wanapum tribe's word for the Ghost Dance. Smohalla was their chief and the leader of their first Ghost Dance.

WIRIKUTA

Means Precious Flower in the Huichol language and is also the name for the sacred place where peyote grows outside the city of San Luis Potosí, Mexico.

WIWAYAK WACIPI

The Lakota Sioux word for the Sun Dance, the seventh and final rite of being human given to them by their messiah White Buffalo Calf Woman.

XAPORI

The Yanomami word for the human spirits of great ancestors who inhabit the shadows of the forest and help maintain its health.

XAWARA

The fumes that a witch makes to cause disease. Many indigenous peoples of the Americas have believed humans to be naturally healthy and that it was the spells of witches that cause disease.

XOCHIQUETZAL

The Aztec name for Precious Flower. She is the goddess of youthful beauty and young love and keeper of the sacred magic of growing plants. She represents the nubile divine feminine.

XOLOTL

The dog god that accompanies the Lord of the Wind on his jouney through the underworld to evolve into the Plumed Serpent. Xolotl is creator of the four directions and a loyal friend, but he is also a lascivious, hairless hound.

YOMAVE

The brother of the Yanomami Lord of Witches, Omave. Like Tezcatlipoca, Yomave also lost his foot to a crocodile. Yomave knows the magic needed to stop the epidemics accidentally brought to them by Omave.

Author's Note: Although mushrooms technically are not plants, for ease of expression at times the word "plants" in the book is used loosely to include fungi.

ACKNOWLEDGEMENTS

It took me almost half a century to learn the story and thirteen years to write *The Ghost Dance*. These are the people who made it possible and with the deepest gratitude, I thank them all: John Fire Lame Deer, the rascally Lakota sage who first taught me about the Ghost Dance. My dear friends, Daniel and Lucia Puledo, who have taken a journey across time with me and over the last half century have taught me a great deal of Mazatecan folklore and history. Roy Stone, Sr., a traditional Lakota healer who allowed me to catch a glimpse of what his people have kept alive. Heather Vuchinich, my loving better half, who edited this book along with the rest of my life. James Walton my scholarly compatriot with whom I have taken the literary journey through the codices. My friend forever, Anina Maurier, who once saved me from dying of malaria and also helped edit this book. Robbie Woliver, whose guidance and literary wisdom helped bring this book to completion. Xapowi, the centenarian headman of the Lechosa Yanomami; by taking me in as his grandson, I gained entry into the Yanomami world of Venezuela's Amazon rain forest. Enrique Lucho and José Valero (the son of famous Chief Fusiwe and kidnapped Brazilian, Helena Valero); for many years, Enrique and José were my traveling companions among the Yanomami. My brilliant friend, the groundbreaking anthropologist and co-founder of Survival International, Francis Huxley, for his deep insight into the book and my soul. Natalie McNamara who suffered through teaching me to write in the beginning. Chaminare, Chief of the Yekuana Tribe of Venezuela's Amazon. Oscar, Chief of the Huambisa Jivaro of Peru. Antonio, Chief of the Venezuelan Piaroa. My partner Francisco Fuentes, retired chief medical officer of the Venezuelan National Guard in the Amazon; in the beginning we fought the epidemics together. Lencho and Erasto Calistro who taught me to survive in the rain forest. Omar Gonzales Nunez, the honorable and courageous head of the Venezuelan Bureau of Indian Affairs. Monica and Scott Pierce, David Wolfberg and Catherine Cooley, staff of the Amazonia Foundation whose hard work allowed me to be present while many of the stories in this book took place. My first goddaughter, Marcella Surra, whose understanding of design and literary media helped make the cover art and this book possible. My goddaughter, Solange Aguilar, for her help with grammatical corrections. Claire Mosher for her computer graphic work and illustrations. Leslie Dinkel who worked with me to help the Yanomami during the epidemics and also to save the lineage of buffalo in North America. Leonard Crow Dog for receiving those pure buffalo and recognizing them for what they are. The Old Turtle who showed me the path into the mystery. And, of course, Desheto for wanting to help humankind and for telling me this story.

ABOUT THE AUTHOR

Michael Stuart Ani and Heather "Fern" Vuchinich

From 1988 to 2002, after many years of jungle training, Michael Stuart Ani and his Amazonia Foundation became a central part of a medical outreach program introduced to fight the epidemics among the Yanomami tribe of Venezuela. In 1992, Michael co-won the "Best of Festival" from the US Environmental Film Festival for *Yanomami: Keepers of the Flame*, which was about the struggle to stop the epidemics. For his efforts, Michael was made a member of the Explorers Club.

He later directed a documentary for the Catalina Island Conservancy entitled *Going Home*, which told the story of the repatriation of some of the last genetically pure American bison to the Lakota people.

Ani lived in Mexico's remote Sierra Mazateca region of Oaxaca from the end of the 1960s through the 1970s and is the only outsider to have ever been allowed into the sacred cloud forests. He still returns to visit with his Mazatecan community to this day. Over the last fifty years, he has followed the Rope of the Dead from the tribes of the Amazon rainforest to the tribes of North America tracking the missing steps of the Ghost Dance along the way.

http://MichaelStuartAni.com

415-306-4752

michaelstuartani@gmail.com

Made in the USA
Columbia, SC
08 June 2019